237
Intimate
Questions

...Every Woman Should Ask a Man

Laura Corn

Park Avenue Publishers

Published by:
Park Avenue Publishers, Inc.
P.O. Box 20010
Oklahoma City, OK 73156

Printed in the United States Of America

ISBN 0-9629628-0-5 :   Softcover

10 9 8 7 6 5 4 3

Cover Photo by: Mizuno
Ms. Corns Photo by: Mizuno
Cover Design by: Laura Corn, Peter Fowler,
William and Francine Blumhoff, Randy and Sheri Small
Page Design/Layout by: Rick Piscitelli
Image Setting by: Icon West
Color Separation by: Western Laser, Icon West
Printed by: Delta Lithograph Co.

This book is printed on recycled paper.

APPRECIATION

I feel very grateful to the many people who, throughout the writing of this book, gave me their love and support.

Ron Keys, thank you, for showing me you never lose when you give love and for planting the seed that knowledge is power.

I want to thank with all my heart my best friend, **Joann Rossi,** without whom this book could not have been written. She gave me the love, and confidence I needed to complete the project. She wrote many of the questions and spent endless hours editing, polishing and bringing to life a vision we both share.

I am forever grateful to **Bill J. Wright,** my publisher, who believed in the project from the beginning. His long hours of editing, work and patience made my dream come true.

I am also deeply grateful to the following people:

Barry Goldwater, Jr. for always leading me to believe I could do and be anything I wanted.

John Dean, for challenging me to be the best.

Mike Curry, for teaching me the sale doesn't begin until they say no.

Jim Arcara, for standing by me and helping me when I needed it the most.

Tim Daze, whose encouragement showed me the true meaning of, "What is a friend?"

David Rolke, Jr. for spiritual growth, beautiful music and total focus.

Linda Seto & Jay Corn: for opening their house to me and showing me love.

John & Cass Corn, for their inspiration and enthusiasm.

A big thanks to the owner's and employees at Hollywood Sheet Music, for allowing me to do month's of research in their store. **Stephen Barber, Stephanie Rinaldo, Don Wonders, Dick Cotterman.** Also a hearty thank you to, **Ralph L. Edwards, Jeff Petersen, Bill Stamps, Robin G. Eisenman, Rico Rossi** and **Dino Rossi, NCNB Bank, Jack Rosner, Jessica Zimmer, Barbara Alvarez, Kim Gilmore, Louise Brooks** and **Bob Flournoy.**

AUTHOR'S NOTES

This book is the product of two years of library research and more than two thousand interviews with men and women from across the country. It began as personal therapy to help me sort out why my marriage had failed and why I didn't enjoy sex.

I do not have formal academic credentials with a string of letters after my name, but I have lived life in the real world in a variety of occupations and circumstances and I know what makes real people hurt.

Through my research and interviews, I discovered what men and women want, indeed, need to know about each other and what they wish their partner would ask. I learned that they are longing to share their thoughts and feelings but, too often, just don't know how to break the silence. There are hundreds of books urging couples to communicate, but they don't give you the words. This book does.

My book is designed to create intimacy and build anticipation between lovers. I have tried to make it fun and entertaining while maintaining a sincere purpose to improve communication and understanding between two people in, or contemplating a relationship.

It can be used alone or shared by a couple. It

can even be the stimulus for a group discussion. However you use it, your personal relationship will benefit by your increased awareness of what other people are thinking. By asking the questions in this book and listening to men's responses I learned how to have a successful relationship and how to enjoy making love.

How and why does it work?

It works, when read alone, because it gives you insight that others are wondering about the same things and having the same doubts, fears, and fantasies. Talk usually turns out better when preceded by at least a modicum of thought and you will be better prepared when it is talking time.

It works, when shared by a couple, because listening is half of communication and is the highest compliment you can pay another. It works because hearing the questions asked with feeling is a soft tease infinitely more exciting than merely reading the text silently. The questions spur warm feelings and create mental images to quicken the pulse and build desire.

It works because information is intimacy, the more information you share, the closer you feel.

The book is arranged in three chapters of Romantic, Sexual, and Mind questions.

ROMANTIC QUESTIONS

The Romantic Questions are introduced by well known song lyrics. Surprisingly, 88% of these predominantly tender and romantic lyrics were written by men which tells me men have been getting a unfair rap when accused of being insensitive. Give them a chance and they will open up. Share the lyrics with your lover, give him time to think about the message before asking the question. The music moves the body, but the lyrics move the soul. The lyrics and questions will trigger memories and fantasies. You will both visualize a potential escapade and be turned on by the playful possibilities. The excitement in this chapter lies in your ability to build anticipation and make the scenes come true.

SEXUAL QUESTIONS

The Sexual Questions are preceded by key excerpts from best selling sexual books, all citing communication, or the lack thereof, as the number one sexual problem. Two people who share their bodies should be able to share their minds. Read the excerpt first, then pose the question without hesitation or embarrassment. An atmosphere of sexual honesty can be unbelievably comfortable and rewarding. Explore all the excerpts and questions in depth. It will pave the way to an irresistible, erotic intimacy and enrich your sex life forever.

MIND QUESTIONS

The Mind Questions are paired with quotes from great, near great, and some completely unknown, thinkers, and philosophers. The introspection forced by these questions will give you a deeper look inside your lover's mind and your own as well.

Ask the questions with a smile in your voice, softness in your eyes, and sincerity in your heart. Your voice becomes an aphrodisiac drawing him to you. Don't hurry or ask too many questions at one sitting. Intimacy takes time. Improvise, ad lib or change the premise of a question. Inevitably, the questions will flow in both directions and that works, too. Try not to challenge his responses. Remember, there are no right or wrong answers, only honest or dishonest ones.

Here are 237 messages to let him know you care. Every answer will reveal something you both need to know and bring you closer together. You will communicate 237 times, creating moments of intimacy with each exchange and becoming best friends as well as lovers.

Enjoy.

Wishing you all the best.

1

Thank Heaven For Little Girls
Alan Jay Lerner

Thank Heaven for little girls
for little girls get bigger everyday.
Thank heaven for little girls
they grow up in the most delightful way.
Those little eyes so helpless and appealing
one day will flash and send you crashing
through the ceiling.
Thank heaven for little girls
for without them what would little boys do?

Do you remember your very first kiss?

Something Good

Richard Rogers

Perhaps I had a wicked childhood,
Perhaps I had a miserable youth.
But somewhere in my wicked miserable past
there must have been a moment of truth.
For here you are, standing there, loving me
whether or not you should.
So, somewhere in my youth or childhood
I must have done something good.

Do you believe soulmates meet by accident or
by destiny?

The Way You Look Tonight
Dorothy Fields

With each word your tenderness grows
Tearing my fear apart.
And that laugh that wrinkles your nose
Touches my foolish heart.
Lovely,
never never change,
Keep that breathless charm,
won't you please arrange it,
cause I love you
Just the way you look tonight
Mmm, mmm
Just the way you look tonight.

What makes a woman unforgettable?

Picnic
Steve Allen

On a picnic morning, without a warning,
I looked at you and somehow I knew.
On a day singing, my heart went winging.
A picnic grove was our rendezvous.

If your rendezvous was a picnic on the bed,
what foods would be in the basket?

Misty
Johnny Burke

Look at me, I'm as helpless as a kitten
up a tree,
and I feel like I'm clinging to a cloud;
I can't understand, I get misty just holding
your hand.

Do you ever lay in the grass side by side
and try to find the same images in the clouds?

Laughter in the Rain
Neil Sedaka / Phil Cody

Strolling along country roads with my baby
it starts to rain, it begins to pour.
Without an umbrella we're soaked to the skin,
I feel a shiver run up my spine.
I feel the warmth of her hand in mine.
Oh, I hear laughter in the rain,
Walking hand and hand with the one I love.
Oooo, how I love the rainy days and
the happy way I feel inside.

When was the last time you took a stroll in
the rain?

Language of the Heart
David Wilcox

We made our warm bed of blankets
in the meadow way up high.
You took off your dress in the moonlight
to sleep beneath the sky.
Your touch was a warm summer ocean!
Your kiss made the whole mountain fly!
And you looked deep within me
and smiled at the tears in my eyes.
Well you say you were always honest
And that your words were clear from the start
But it was more than words that got spoken
There was language of the heart.

When you look deep within your lover's eyes,
what do you hope you'll see?

Sunday Kind of Love

Barbara Belle / Louis Prim / Anita Leonard / Stan Rhodes

I want a Sunday kind of love
a love to last past Saturday night,
I'd like to know that it's more than
love at first sight.
I want a Sunday kind of love.
I do all my Sunday dreaming
and all my Sunday scheming
every minute, every hour, every day.
And I'm hoping to discover
a certain kind of lover
who will show me the way.
I want a Sunday kind of love.

What is a Sunday kind of love?

Send One Your Love

Stevie Wonder

I know people say
two hearts beating as one is unreal and can
only happen in make believe stories.
But so blind they all must be that they cannot
believe what they see,
for around us are miracles of love's glory.
Send her your love with a dozen roses;
Make sure she knows it
with a flower from your heart
Show him your love,
don't hold back your feeling's
you don't need a reason
when it's straight from your heart.

Sending flowers is one way to show your love,
what are four other ways?

Always On My Mind
Wayne Carson Head / Johnny Christopher / Mark James

Maybe I didn't love you
quite as often as I could have.
And maybe I didn't treat you
quite as good as I should have.
If I made you feel second best
girl, I am sorry I have tried.
You were always on my mind
You were always on my mind.

Why is it hard for you to show your
true feelings?

If I Loved You

Oscar Hammerstein II

If I loved you, time and again I would
try to say all I'd want you to know.
If I loved you, words wouldn't come in an
easy way, 'round in circles I'd go.
Longin' to tell you, but afraid and shy,
I'd let my golden chances pass me by!
Soon you'd leave me,
off you would go in the midst of day,
never, never to know how I loved you
If I loved you.

If you love someone, how often should you
say the words?

You Should Hear How She Talks About You
Dean Pitchford

You should hear how she talks about you.
You should hear what she said.
She says she would be lost without you
She's half out of her head.
You should hear how she talks about you
She just can't get enough
She says she would be lost without you
She is really in love.

How do you talk about the woman in your life
when you're not with her?

Nearness of You

Ned Washington

Why do I just wither and forget all resistance
when you and your magic pass by?
My heart's in a dither, dear, when you're at a
distance but when you are near,
Oh, My!

What do you think about when you touch a
woman's inner thigh?

Close The Door
Kenneth Gamble / Leon Huff

Close the door
let me give you what you've been waiting for
I've got so much love to give
and I'm going to give it all to you.
Please close the door
let me rub your back that you say is sore.

If she has had a long day at work and her body
aches, would you tell her to lie on the bed while
you give her a rub down with warm scented oil?

Can you do this for her pleasure alone, without
letting her know how much you're turned-on
sexually?

She Touched Me

Ira Levin

> She touched me, she put her hand near mine
> and then she touched me.
> I felt a sudden tingle when she touched me,
> a sparkle a glow!
> I simply have to face the fact, she touched me,
> control myself and try to act as if I remember
> my name.
> But she touched me, she touched me,
> and suddenly nothing is the same!

How can a woman touch you like you've never
been touched before?

After the Lovin'

Ernesto Phillips

So I sing you to sleep
After the lovin'
I brush back the hair from your eyes.
And the love on your face is so real
That it makes me want to cry.
I know that my song isn't saying
anything new;
Oh, but after the lovin'
I'm still in love with you.

After you make love, while you are falling asleep,
do you like to feel your lover's body touching yours?
If so, what part of her body comforts you the most?

My Cup Runneth Over

Tom Jones

> Sometimes in the morning when shadows
> are deep
> I lie here beside you just watching you sleep
> And sometimes I whisper what I'm thinking of
> My cup runneth over with love.

If you were going to whisper something in your lover's ear while she lay asleep, something she has never heard from you before, what would it be?

Wicked Game

Chris Issac

What a wicked game you play
to make me feel this way
What a wicked thing to do
to make me dream of you
What a wicked thing to say
you never felt this way
What a wicked thing to do
to make me dream of you

If you could watch your lover do something,
without her being aware of it, what would it be?

That's Enough For Me

Paul Williams

> If I can make you cry
> If I can fill your eyes with pleasure
> Just by holding you
> In the early hours of mornin'
> When the day that lies ahead's
> Not quite begun.
> Oh, well, that's enough for me
> That's all the hero I need to be
> I smile to think of you and me
> You and I
> And how our pleasure makes you cry.

If you are held and loved in the early morning hours, in what ways does your day seem to be filled with greater pleasure?

I Say A Little Prayer
Hal David

The moment I get up,
before I get shaved and set up
I say a little prayer for you.
While combing my hair now
and wondering what tie to wear now
I say a little prayer for you.

When you say a little prayer for the one you love,
what do you pray for?

The Sweetheart Tree

Johnny Mercer

They say there's a tree in the forest
a tree that will give you a sign,
Come along with me, to the sweetheart tree,
come and carve your name next to mine.

It's a soft, summer kind of day, the grass is green and lush, you grab a blanket from the car and take her hand. Would you stop under the first tree or would you search for just the right one? If you carved a love message in the bark, what would it say?

Lollipops And Roses
Tony Velona

Tell her you care each time you speak.
Make it her birthday each day of the week.
Bring her nice things, sugar and spice things,
roses and lollipops and lollipops and roses.
We try acting grown up, but as a rule
we're all little children fresh from school.
So carry her books. That's how it starts.
Fourteen or forty they're kids in their hearts.

How does it make *you* feel when you surprise her
with little unexpected gifts?

Woman
John Lennon

Woman I know you understand
the little child inside the man
Please remember my life is in your hands.

In what ways do you remain the little boy inside
the man?

You Make Me Feel So Young
Mack Gordon

Do I seem as cheerful as a school boy
playing hookey?
Do I seem to gurgle like a baby
with a cookie?
If I do, the cause of it all is you.
You make me feel so young,
You make me feel spring has sprung.
And everytime I see you grin,
I'm such a happy individual.
The moment you speak
I wanna go play hide and seek.
I wanna go bounce the moon,
just like a toy balloon.
You make me feel so young.

How old would you be if you didn't know how old
you were?

Chevy Van
Sammy Johns

Like a picture she was laying there
moonlight dancing off her hair.
She woke up and took me by the hand
she's gonna love me in my Chevy Van.

If she were going to make love to you on lovers
lane, what kind of car would you drive to
the moonlight?

Make Me Lose Control

Eric Carmen / Dean Pitchford

We put the top down and parked
beneath the moon in the sky,
and the wind is so hard in our hair
like a fire in July;
Jennifer's singin' "Stand By Me"
and she knows every single word by heart;
was love always this good
or could this be just the start.
Oh, darlin', turn the radio up
for that sweet sound;
hold me close never let me go,
take me over the edge
make me lose control.

Name one song to which you know every single
word by heart . . . why are these lyrics so special
to you?

Let's Misbehave

Cole Porter

We're all alone no chapter one,
can get our number,
the world's in a slumber,
Let's Mis-be-have.
There's something wild about you child,
That's so con-ta-gious,
Let's Mis-be-have.

You're holding hands as you walk along a
deserted beach; suddenly she takes off
all of her clothes and jumps into the water,
what will you do?

Under The Boardwalk
Arthur Resnick / Kenny Young

Under the boardwalk down by the sea
On a blanket with my baby's where I'll be.
Under the boardwalk out of the sun.
Under the boardwalk we'll be having some fun.
Under the boardwalk people walkin' around
Under the boardwalk we'll be falling in love.

Where is the zaniest, most unusual place you
would like to make love. . .but haven't?

'Til I Kissed You
Don Everly

Never felt like this until I kissed you.
How did I exist until I kissed you?
Never had you on my mind,
now you're there all the time
Never knew what I missed until I kissed you.

What's your favorite type of kiss?

Peaceful Easy Feeling

Jack Tempchin

I like the way your sparkling earrings lay
against your skin so brown.
And I wanna sleep with you in the desert
tonight with a billion stars all around.
'Cause I got a peaceful easy feeling
and I know you won't let me down.

When was the last time you made love outdoors
with a billion stars all around? Where, in a
beautiful, romantic, outdoor setting, would you
choose to sleep with your lover?

MoonDance

Van Morrison

Well, it's a marvelous night for a moondance
with the stars up-above in your eyes,
A fab-tabul-ous night to make romance
'neath the cover of October skies.
And all the leaves on the trees are falling
to the sound of the breezes that blow;
And I'm trying to please to the calling
of your heart strings that play soft and low.
Can I just have one more moondance
with you, my love?

If you were going to choreograph your lovemaking
to a type of dance, what would it be?

Incurably Romantic

Sammy Cahn

I'm susceptible to stars in the skies,
I'm incurably romantic.
If they're told to me all covered with
sighs the wildest of lies seem true.
Each time a love bird sings
I have no defenses,
My heart is off on wings
Along with my senses.
I'm set up for the moon
when it's bright, I'm incurably romantic,
and I shouldn't be allowed out at night
with anyone quite like you.
But oh! your arms are nice,
and it would be awfully nice if you
turned out to be starry eyed like me,
and in-cur-a-bly ro-man-tic too!

What would you prescribe for someone who is
"Incurably Romantic"?

You Do Something To Me

Cole Porter

You do something to me
Something that simply mys-ti-fies me.
Tell me, why should it be you have
the power to hypnotize me?
Let me live 'neath your spell,
do do that voo-doo that you do so well.
For you do something to me that
nobody else could do.

If you were to pick the one alluring quality
that draws you to a woman and keeps you there,
what would it be?

In Search of the Perfect Shampoo
Michael Franks

You threw me, you walked right up to me
My fol-li-cles prayed it was true.
We're pure organic; no more
med-i-cat-ed goo.
Now I've found me the perfect
Sham-poo— and it's you.
So rub-a-dub-dub-dub,
just you and me in the tub . . .
gonna suds away all our troubles
in a million low pH Bubbles.

If you were going to wash her hair, what scent
of shampoo would you use?

Young At Heart
Carolyn Leigh

Fairy tales can come true,
it can happen to you
If you're Young at Heart!
For it's hard you will find,
to be narrow of mind
If you're Young at Heart!
You can go to extremes
with impossible schemes,
You can laugh when your dreams
fall apart at the seams,
And life gets more exciting
with each passing day
and love is either in your heart or on the way
If you're Young at Heart!

Could you go to an ice cream parlor and share a
banana split filled with juicy fruits, chocolate
sauces, and whipped cream, feed each other and
feel sexy about it? What is the silliest, most
"young at heart" thing you can think of that you
would like to do?

Annie's Song
John Denver

You fill up my senses
Like a night in the forest,
Like the mountains in spring time,
Like a walk in the rain,
Like a storm in the desert,
Like a sleepy blue ocean
You fill up my senses
Come fill me again.

What is the most romantic sensation you have
ever experienced?

All Shook Up
Elvis Presley / Otis Blackwell

My hands are shaky and my knees are weak,
I can't seem to stand on my own two feet,
Who do you thank when you have such luck?
I'm in love!
I'M ALL SHOOK UP!

When you're in love, do you *walk* differently?

Both To Each Other (Friends & Lovers)
Jay Gruska / Paul Gordon

What would you say if I told you
I've always wanted to hold you
I don't know what we're afraid of;
nothin' would change of we made love.
'Cause I'll be your friend, and I'll be your lover
Well, I know in our heart we agree
we don't have to be one or the other.
No, we could be both to each other.

Do you believe that for love to last, you must be
both a best friend and a lover? Which is more
important, to be friends first or lovers first?

Sailing
Christopher Cross

Well, it's not far down to paradise
at least it's not for me.
And if the wind is right, you can sail away
and find tranquility.
Oh, the canvas can do miracles,
just you wait and see
Believe me.
Sailing takes me away
to where I've always heard it could be
Just a dream and the wind to carry me
and soon I will be free.

When you need tranquility, where do you find it?

Weekend In New England

Randy Edelman

Time in New England took me away
to long rocky beaches and you by the bay.
We started a story whose end must now wait.
And tell me,
When will our eyes meet?
When can I touch you?
When will this strong yearning end?
And when will I see you again?

How much absence should there be in a
relationship to keep the heart growing fonder?

Anticipation

Carly Simon

> We can never know about the days to come
> But we can think about them anyway.
> And I wonder if I'm really with you now,
> Or just chasing after some finer day.
> An-tic-i-pa-tion,
> An-tic-i-pa-tion is making me late,
> is keeping me wait————ing.

What is your favorite type of romantic
Anticipation?

Unchained Melody
Hy Zaret

Oh, my love my darling
I've hungered for your touch
a long lonely time.
Time, goes by, so slowly,
and time can do so much
Are you——still mine?
I need your love
I need your love
God speed your love
to me.

When you're away from your lover, how often
do you wonder if she is thinking about you?
What do you miss most when you're apart?

Don't Make Me Over

Hal David

Don't make me over,
now that I can't make it
without you.
Don't make me over
I wouldn't change one thing about you.
Don't pick on the things I say,
the things I do
Just love me with all my faults
the way that I love you.
I'm begging you
Don't make me over.

Can you love and accept all sides of a woman
with no desire to make her over?

All The Man That I Need
Dean Pitchford / Michael Gore

In the morning when I kiss his eyes,
he takes me down, he rocks me slow.
And in the evening when the moon is high,
he holds me close and won't let go
He won't let go.
He fills me up
He gives me love,
More love than I've ever seen.
He's all I got
He's all I've got in this world,
but he's all the man I need.

Do you believe behind every happy woman
there is the love of a good man? What do you
think a woman needs to be fulfilled?

She's a Lady
Paul Anka

Well, she's all you'd ever want,
She's the kind men like to flaunt
and take to dinner.
Well, she always knows her place,
She's got style, she's got grace
She's a winner.
She's a Lady.

When you go to dinner, do you like to find out
what the lady wants and order it for her?

You Go To My Head
Haven Gillespie

> You go to my head
> And you linger like a haunting refrain
> And I feel you spinning 'round in my brain
> like the bubbles in a glass of champagne.
> You go to my head.

When you are sharing a bottle of wine or champagne, do you like to make one toast or several? What similarities are there between champagne and being in love?

People Will Say We're In Love
Oscar Hammerstein ll

Don't throw bouquets at me
Don't please my folks too much
Don't laugh at my jokes too much
People will say we're in love!
Don't sigh and gaze at me
Your sighs are so like mine.
Your eyes mustn't glow like mine
People will say we're in love!

While out in public, what kind of affection
do you enjoy from your lover?

Physical

Terry Shaddick

I've been patient
I've been good
Trying to keep my hands on the table
It's getting hard, this holding back
You know what I mean?
Let's get physical, physical
I wanna get physical, let me hear
your body talk.

When you're out for dinner, do you prefer to
sit across the table from the one you're with
or sit side by side?

I Had The Time Of My Life

Frank Previte / Donald Markowitz / John Denicola

Remember,
You're the one thing I can't get enough of.
So I'll tell you something
This could be love, because
I had the time of my life.
I never felt like this before
I swear it's the truth
And I owe it all to you.

How often do you like to surprise her and make plans for the evening without telling her?

Lover
Lorenz Hart

Lover, when I'm near you
and I hear you speak my name
softly in my ear you breathe a flame.
Lover, when we're dancing,
keep on glancing in my eyes
'til love's own entrancing music dies.

What effect does hearing your name
spoken softly in your ear have on you?

Keep The Candle Burning

Aime Ulrich Rankin / Max Gale

Keep the candle burning
Never lose the light.
Keep the love - wheels turning
Hold the dream inside.
Keep the candle burning
Keep the feeling alive.

When you see candles burning in the bedroom,
what kind of feelings does it kindle inside?

Chances Are
Al Stillman

Chances are 'cause I wear a silly grin,
The moment you come into view,
Chances are, you think I'm in love with you.
Just because my composure sort of slips,
The moment that your lips meet mine,
Chances are you think my heart's your
Valentine.

If you made a pact to celebrate Valentine's Day
once a week for the next year, what day would
you choose?

Smoke Gets In Your Eyes
Otto Harbach / Jerome Kern

They asked me how I knew my love was true?
I of course replied,
"Something here inside cannot be denied."
They said someday you'll find, all who love
are blind.
When your heart's on fire, you must realize
Smoke gets in your eyes.

After you make love, does the smoke stay in your eyes or do you see crystal clear?

Addicted To Love
Robert Palmer

You like to think you're immune to the stuff
That you can't get enough
Well you might as well face it
Your addicted to love!

If you're addicted to love, what is it that you can't
get enough of?

Great Balls of Fire
Otis Blackwell / Jack Hammer

You shake my nerves and you rattle my brain
Too much love drives a man insane
You broke my will but what a thrill
Goodness gracious great balls of fire!

Can too much love drive a man insane?

(Love is like a) Heatwave
Edward Holland / Lamont Dozier / Brian Holland

Whenever I'm with him
Something inside starts burning
And I'm filled with desire
Could it be just the devil in me
or is this the way love's suppose to be?
It's like a heat-wave
Burning in my heart
I can't keep from crying
It's tearing me apart.

How would you define *too much love*?

More Than You Know
Edward Eliscu / William Rose

More than you know more than you know
man of my heart I love you so.
Lately I find you're on my mind,
more than you know.
Whether you're right whether you're wrong,
man of my heart I'll string along.
You need me so, more than you'll ever know.

Do you think it's *wise* to love someone
more than they know?
How much love are you comfortable with?

Don't Hold Back Your Love
Richard Page / David Tyson / Gerald O'Brien

Don't hold back your love
I know it's here;
I wanna see it come to life
before my eyes.
Don't hold back your love
Show me your heart cause I will always
be here by your side.
One more chance to find a higher ground
One more chance before the curtains down
One more night to turn your life around
No, don't hold back your love.

When you make love do you let go completely
or do you hold back just a little?

Lay Lady Lay
Bob Dylan

Lay Lady Lay
Lay across my big brass bed.
Stay Lady Stay
Stay with your man for awhile.

What makes a lady a *lady*?

You Stepped Out Of A Dream
Gus Kahn

You stepped out of a dream
You are too wonderful to be what you seem!
Could there be eyes like yours
Could there be lips like yours,
Could there be smiles like yours,
honest and truly?
You stepped out of a dream.

When does a woman's face look the most
beautiful to you?

Crackers

Rhonda Fleming / Dennis Morgan

You can eat crackers in my bed anytime, baby
You can kick off the covers in the middle
of the night
You can sleep with the window open wide,
Do anything as long as you're by my side.
Oooh baby,
You can eat crackers in my bed anytime!

What do you like to eat between the sheets?

Our House
Graham Nash

Staring at the fire for hours and hours
while I listen to you play your love songs
all night long for me, only for me.
Our house is a very, very, very fine house.
With two cats in the yard,
life used to be so hard
Now everything is easy 'cause of you.

I'll light the fire, while you place the
flowers in the vase that you bought today.

What is your favorite room in the house?

Afternoon Delight
Bill Danoff

Thinkin' of you is workin' up an appetite
Lookin' forward to a little afternoon delight
The thought of lovin' you is getting so exciting
Sky Rockets in flight . . . Afternoon delight!

How would you plan an intimate rendezvous
for a little afternoon delight?

I Don't Stand A Ghost Of A Chance With You

Ned Washington / Bing Crosby

If you'd surrender
for a tender kiss or two.
You might discover
that I'm the lover meant for you.

Do you surrender to soft, warm, unpredictable kisses? When she's kissing you gently, what emotions do you feel?

Take My Breath Away
Tom Witlock

Watching every move in this
foolish lover's game.
Watching you in slow motion
as you turn around and say,
"Take my breath away,
My love
Take my breath away."

When she kisses your lips and then breathes
deeply into your mouth, do you take her breath
away and then give her yours?

Lady In Red
Chris DeBarge

I've never seen you looking so
gorgeous as you did tonight;
I've never seen you shine so bright
You were amazing.
I've never seen so many
people want to be there by your side
and when you turned to me and smiled,
it took my breath away.
I have never had such a feeling
Such a feeling of complete and utter love
As I do tonight
The lady in red is dancing with me.

What color is passion? What color is love?
What color is intimacy?

Forever in Blue Jeans
Neil Diamond / Richard Bennett

Money talks,
but it don't sing and dance and it don't walk
And long as I can have you here with me
I'd much rather be
forever in blue jeans.

If a woman had to wear the same clothes for an entire week what would you like to see her wear?

68

Good Vibrations
Brian Wilson

I love the colorful clothes she wears
and the way the sunlight plays upon her hair.
I hear the sound of a gentle word
on the wind that lifts her perfume
through the air.

Do the clothes make the woman or does the
woman make the clothes?

Mister Sandman
Pat Ballard

Mister Sandman, bring me a dream
Make her complexion like peaches and cream.
Give her two lips like roses in clover,
Then tell me that my lonesome nights
are over.
Please turn on your magic beam,
Mister Sandman, bring me a dream.

If Mr. Sandman were a blindman, how would you describe the female body to him?

How Sweet It Is To Be Loved By You
Edward Holland / Lamont Dozier / Brian Holland

I wanna stop and thank you baby,
I just wanna stop and thank you, baby
How sweet it is to be loved by you.

How often do you stop what you're doing and
take time out for a kiss?

Old Cape Cod
Claire Rothrock / Mitt Yakers / Allan Jeffery

If you're fond of sand dunes and salty air,
Quaint little villages here and there;
You're sure to fall in love with old Cape Cod.
If you like the taste of lobster stew,
Served by a window with an ocean view;
You're sure to fall in love with old Cape Cod.

What are the most romantic cities in America?

I Love To See You Smile
Randy Newman

I was born to make you happy
I think you're just my style
Everywhere I go, tell everyone I know
baby, I love to see you smile.
In the springtime, winter or fall
the only place I'd want to be is
where I can see you smile at me.
In a world full of trouble
You make it all worth-while
What would I do if I didn't have you?
I just love to see you smile.

When the woman you love smiles at you,
how does that make you feel?

Round Midnight
Bernie Hanighen

When some quarrel we had needs mending
Does it mean our love is ending
Darling I need you
lately I find
When you're out of my arms
I'm out of my mind.

Sometime during the day you and your lover
have a quarrel. Would you go to bed with bad
feelings or would you take the time to set things
right between you?

Sometimes When We Touch

Dan Hill / Berry Mann

Sometimes when we touch
the honesty's too much
I have to close my eyes and hide.
I want to hold you 'til I die
'til we both break down and cry
I want to hold you 'til the fear in me subsides.

What is it about love that makes you afraid?

I Only Have Eyes For You
Al Dubin

My love must be a kind of blind love
I can't see anyone but you.
I don't know if we're in a garden
or a crowded avenue.
Maybe millions of people go by
but they all disappear from view,
And I only have eyes for you!

When you're out with a lady, do you only
have eyes for her? Do you expect her to
only have eyes for you?

When Your Hair has Turned To Silver
Charlie Tobias / Peter DeRose

When your hair has turned to silver
I will love you just the same;
I will only call you sweetheart,
That will always be your name
Through a garden filled with roses
Down the street trail we'll stray
When your hair has turned to silver
I will love you as today.

When her hair has turned to silver, will you still
call her sweetheart?

Wishin' On A Star
Billie Calvin

I'm wishin' on a star
to follow where you are.
I'm wishin' on a dream
to follow what it means.
And I wish on all the rainbows that I see
I wish on all the people who really dream.

Would you be more likely to be wishin' on
a star, at the end of a rainbow, on a wishbone
or in a wishing well? What would you wish
for if she were holding your hand?

Blue Moon

Lorenz Hart

Blue Moon you saw me standing alone
Without a dream in my heart
Without a love of my own.

Blue Moon you knew just what I was there for
You heard me saying a prayer for
Someone I really could care for.

In what ways do you feel different when there's
a full moon?

You'd Be So Nice To Come Home To
Cole Porter

You'd be so nice to come home to,
You'd be so nice by the fire,
While the breeze, on high, sang a lullaby,
You'd be all that I could desire.

You have an evening with everything connected
to romance working for you, it's been several
hours, she falls asleep while in your arms in
front of the fire and you don't make love, do
you feel disappointed?

A Lovely Way To Spend An Evening
Jimmy McHugh

This is a lovely way to spend an evening
Can't think of anything I'd rather do.
This is a lovely way to spend an evening
Can't think of anyone as lovely as you.
A casual stroll thru a garden,
a kiss by a lazy lagoon
Catching a breath of moonlight,
humming our favorite tune.

What is your favorite way to spend an evening?

I'll Have To Say I Love You In A Song
Jim Croce

Yeah, I know it's kind of strange
But everytime I'm near you
I just run out of things to say
I know you'd understand.
Everytime the time was right
The words just came out wrong
So I'll have to say I love you in a song!

If you couldn't think of anything to say and you
wanted to tell her that you love her in a song,
what song would you play?

With You I'm Born Again
Carol Conners

Come bring your softness
comfort me through all this madness
Woman, don't you know with you
I'm Born Again.

Come give me your sweetness
with you there is no weakness
Lying safe within your arms
I'm Born Again.

After making love, would you cradle her in
your arms or have her cradle you in hers?

Heart and Soul
Frank Loesser

Heart and Soul I fell in love with you
Heart and Soul the way a fool would do madly
Because you held me tight
and stole a kiss in the night.
Heart and Soul.

Do you like to steal kisses and squeezes through
the night?

He Calls Me Crazy
Bob Russell

I say I'll move the mountains
And I'll move the mountains
If he wants them out of the way.
Crazy he calls me
Sure I'm crazy
Crazy in love I'd say.

On a crazy romantic spur of the moment you
might . . .

Poetry Man
Phoebe Snow

> You're a Genie
> All I ask for is your smile each time
> I rub the lamp.
> When I am with you, I have a giggling
> teenage crush though I'm a sultry vamp,
> Yeah a sultry vamp.
>
> Oh, talk to me some more
> You don't have to go
> You're the poetry man
> You make things all rhyme.

If she whispered in your ear,
"You give my thighs butterflies."
what would you whisper in her ear?

Abracadabra

Steve Miller

> I feel the magic in your caress
> I feel the magic when I touch your dress;
> Silk and satin, leather and lace;
> Black panties with an angel's face.

If she did a slow, soft, sensuous strip tease
for you and left one thing on, what would it be?

Mockingbird

Inez Foxx / Charlie Foxx

Oh, everybody have you heard
he's going to buy me a mockingbird
And if that mockingbird don't sing
he's going to buy me a diamond ring
And if that diamond ring don't shine
he's going to break this heart of mine.

When you buy your girl a gift, does it take you
ten minutes or two hours?

Big Spender
Dorothy Fields

The minute you walked in the joint
I could see you were a man of distinction,
a real big spender
good looking, so refined.
Say wouldn't you like to know
what's going on in my mind?
So let me get right to the point,
I don't pop my cork for every guy I see.
Hey Big Spender!
Spend a little time with me.

Would you ever give your credit card to your lover for an afternoon shopping spree? Would you give her a limit or trust her judgement?

There is Love
The Bible

> Well a man shall leave his mother
> and a woman shall leave her home.
> They shall travel on to where
> the two should be as one.
> As it was in the beginning
> is now and 'til the end
> Woman draws her life from man
> and gives it back again.
> And there is Love.

What is your interpretation of the lyric:
"Woman draws her life from man and
gives it back again. And there is Love."?

Cherry Lips
Winfield Scott

Cherry lips, cherry lips
sweet as sugar cane
Kiss me, kiss me
'til I feel no pain.
Cherry lips, cherry lips
you're red as wine,
Oooh, cherry lips say you'll be mine!

What's your *favorite flavor* of lips?

April Showers
B.G. DeSilva

Though April showers may come your way,
they bring the flowers that bloom in May;
So if it's raining have no regrets
because it isn't raining rain you know,
it's raining violets.

Have you ever gone searching for a field of
flowers to stroll through and make love in?

The Rose
Amanda McBroom

Some say love
it is a razor that leaves the soul to bleed.
Some say love
it is a hunger an endless aching need.
I say love
it is a flower and you its only seed.

If you were the seed and she were the flower,
what flower did you grow?

For The Good Times

Kris Kristofferson

Lay your head upon the pillow,
hold your warm and tender body close to mine.
Hear the whisper of the raindrops
blowing soft against the window
And make believe you love me one more time.
For the good times.

How many times have you felt your heart break?

Making Love
Burt Bacharach / Carol Bayer Sayer

Here, close to our feelings we touch again,
we love again,
Remember when we thought our hearts
would never mend
and we're all the better for each other.
There's more to love I know,
than Making Love.

Did you ever feel after a broken heart that your
heart would never mend?

There's A Tear In My Beer
Hank Williams, Jr.

There's a tear in my beer
'cause I'm crying for you, dear.
You are on my lonely mind
Into these last 9 beers
I have shed a million tears.

I'm gonna keep on sittin' here until I'm petrified
And maybe these tears will leave my eyes.
There's a tear in my beer
'cause I'm crying over you.

How many tears have you shed in your beer
over a woman?

Don't Cry
Geoffry Downes / John Wetton

Don't cry; now that I've found you
Don't cry; take a look around you
Don't cry; it took so long to find you
Do what you want, but little darling,
Please don't cry.

Do you wipe her tears away with kisses
when she cries?

You Needed Me
Randy Goodrum

I cried a tear, you wiped it dry.
I was confused, you cleared my mind.
I sold my soul, you bought it back for me
And held me up and gave me dignity
Somehow you needed me.

You gave me strength to stand alone again
To face the world out on my own again.
You put me high upon a ped-es-tal
So high that I can almost see e-ter-ni-ty,
Somehow you needed me,
You needed me.

How important is it for you to feel needed?

Speak Softly Love
Larry Kusih

Speak softly love, and hold me
warm against your heart
When I feel your words, the tender,
trembling moments start.
We're in a world our very own,
Sharing a love that only a few
have ever known.

Do your legs get weak and your heart skip a beat
when your lover speaks softly?

That Old Black Magic

Johnny Mercer / Harold Arlen

For you're the lover I have waited for.
The mate that fate had me created for
And every time your lips meet mine
Darling down and down I go,
Round and round I go
In a spin,
Loving the spin I'm in
Under that old black magic called love!

What is the highest compliment you can pay
your lover?

It's The Strangest Thing
Fred Ebb

I'll have my back to the door,
Be standing with my back to the door
Yet I'll know when he walks in
It's the strangest thing.
I'll hear the laugh of the crowd,
Though standing well apart from the crowd,
And I'll know when he joins in
It's the strangest thing
What do you suppose it is
that's mine and his?
What would you call that?

All I know when I hear the telephone
ring, as I hurry to answer the ring,
If I know it's him, it's him.
It's the strangest thing.

When the telephone rings, as you answer the
ring, how often do you *know* it's her?
If the two of you go for a long drive and there
is silence for more than an hour, do you feel
uneasy or do you *know* it's just quiet time?

Will We Ever Know Each Other
Martin Charnin

Will we ever know each other well enough?
Get to grow and get to show enough?
There are a thousand things that please you
There are a thousand more that throw you
Babe; I damned well better know you
better than I know you.
You'll love waking up beside me
You'll love the way I velvet glove you
Babe; I damned well better like you
better than "I love you."

What is the difference between liking your
lover and loving your lover?

In a Sentimental Mood
Irving Mills / Manny Kurtz

In a sentimental mood
I can see the stars come thru my room
While your loving attitude
Is like a flame that lights the gloom.
On the wings of every kiss
Drifts a mel-o-dy so strange and sweet
In this sentimental bliss
You make my paradise complete.

When a sentimental mood comes in your room,
what usually causes it?

When Something Is Wrong With My Baby
Isaac Hayes / David Porter

When something is wrong with my baby,
something is wrong with me
And if I know that she's worried,
I know I'd feel the same misery.
We've been through so much together
We stand as one, that's what makes it better
When something is wrong with my baby
Something is wrong with me.

When something is wrong with your baby,
how does it affect you?

Try A Little Tenderness
Jimmy Campbell / Reg Connelly / Harry Woods

In the hustle of the day
we're all inclined to miss
little things that mean so much,
a word, a smile, a kiss.
When a woman loves a man,
he's a hero in her eyes,
and a hero he can always be,
if he'll just realize;
She may get weary, women do get weary,
wearing the same shabby dress,
and when she gets weary
Try a little tenderness.

When your woman is weary, women do get weary,
what do you "try" to do to make her feel better?

I Just Called To Say I Love You
Stevie Wonder

I just called to say, "I love you."
I just called to say how much I care
I just called to say, "I love you."
And I mean it from the bottom of my heart.

How often do you call just to say, "I love you."?

I'm A Woman
Jerry Leiber / Mike Stoller

> If you come to me sickly,
> You know I'm gonna make you well.
> If you come to me hexed up,
> You know I'll break the spell.
> If you come to me hungry,
> You know I'm gonna fill you full of grits.
> If it's lovin' you're lackin'
> I'll kiss you and give you the shiverin' fits!
> I'm a woman!
> W-O-M-A-N
> I'll say it again
> Yes, I'm a WOMAN
> And that's all!

If you were a woman, what occupation
would you be in?

How Lovely To Be a Woman
Lee Adams

How lovely to be a woman
The waiting was well worth while;
How lovely to wear mascara and
smile a woman's smile.
How lovely to have a figure
That's round instead of flat;
Whenever you hear boys whistle,
you're what they're whistling at.

What goes through your mind when you
whistle at a woman?

What's New?
Johnny Burke

What's new?
How is the world treating you?
You haven't changed a bit;
lovely as ever, I must admit.
What's new?
How did that romance come through?
We haven't met since then,
Gee! But it's nice to see you again.

When you've seen or run into an old lover,
did you get that old feeling back again?

Feel Like Making Love
Eugene McDaniels

Strolling through the park
watching winter turn to spring.
Walking through the dark
seeing lovers do their thing.
Oh, that's the time
when I feel like making love to you.
Oh, that's the time
when I feel like making dreams come true.

If you were strolling through the park and came
upon a man and a woman making love and they
couldn't see you, would you watch for a second or
would you be too embarrassed?

It Had To Be You
Gus Kahn

It had to be you
It had to be you
I wandered around and finally found
the somebody who could make me be true,
could make me be blue
and even be glad, just to be sad,
thinking of you.
It had to be you.

Do you believe there "has to be" a perfect
someone for everyone?

When Doves Cry
Prince

> Picture you and I engaged in a kiss
> The sweat of your body covers me.
> Can you, my darling can you picture this?

While making love on a hot sweltering afternoon your sweat begins to drip onto your lover; does this add to the excitement or make you feel uncomfortable?

Close the Door
Kenneth Gamble / Leon Huff

Let's shower together
shower together
I'll wash your body
you'll wash mine.
Rub me down with some hot oils
And I'll do the same for you.

Would you like her to *unexpectedly* jump in the
shower with you to soap you up and wash
you down?

A Lover's Question

Brook Benton / Jimmy Williams

I'd like to know when she's not with me
Is she still true to me?
I'd like to know when we're kissing
does she feel just what I feel and how
am I to know it's really real?
Oh, tell me where the answer lies?
In her kiss or in her eyes?
It's a lover's question,
I'd like to know.

Is love's answer in your kiss or in your eyes?

Nobody Does It Better

Carol Bayer Sayer

Nobody does it better
Makes me feel sad for the rest
Nobody does it half as good as you
Baby, baby, you're the best!

What is it that you do that nobody else
does better?

When Doves Cry
Prince

> Dream, if you can a courtyard
> An ocean of violets in bloom
> Animals strike curious poses
> They feel the heat, the heat
> between me and you.

If you were at the zoo with a date on a sunny
spring day and it was mating season, would
your sexuality be aroused?

Behind Closed Doors
Kenny O'Dell

And when we get behind closed doors
then she lets her hair hang down,
And she makes me glad that I'm a man.
Oh, no one knows what goes on
behind closed doors.

When you get behind closed doors, do you play all
the games you want to play?

Sixty Minute Man
William Ward

There'll be fifteen minutes of kissing
Then you'll hollar please don't stop
(Don't Stop!)
Fifteen minutes of pleasin'
Fifteen minutes of squeezin'
And fifteen minutes of blowing my top!
I'm the Sixty Minute Man.

If you were going to make love for sixty minutes,
how much time would you spend on kissin',
squeezin' and pleasin'?

Do That To Me One More Time
Toni Tennille

Pass that by me one more time
Once is never enough for my heart to hear.
Tell it to me one more time
I can never hear enough while I got you near.
Oh, say those words again like you just did
Oh baby, tell it to me once again.

What words do you like to hear whispered in
your ear over and over and over again?

Slow Hand

John Bettis / Michael Clark

> You want a man with a slow touch,
> You want a lover with an easy touch,
> You want somebody who will spend some time,
> Not come and go in a heated rush.
> Baby, believe me, I understand
> When it comes to love,
> You want a slow hand.

When you caress a woman's body and you're not in a rush, what type of *touch* do you have?

The Secret Garden
Quincy Jones / Rod Temperton / Siedah Garrett / El DeBarge

Tell me a secret.
I don't just wanna about any secret of yours
I wanna know one special secret . . . Oh!
Because, tonight I want to learn all about
the secrets . . . in your garden.
I wanna be with you
Let me lay beside you,
do what you want me to do all night.
Gonna hold you. Oooh, baby
Can I touch you there?
Come on make it allright.
Here in the garden where
temptation feels so right.

What kind of music best describes how your body
moves when you make love?

How Do You Keep The Music Playing?
Allan and Marilyn Bergman

How do you keep the music playing?
How do you make it last?
How do you keep the song from fading too fast?
How do you lose yourself to someone
and never lose your way?
How do you not run out of new things to say?

How do you keep the music playing?

Sexual
Questions

Sex Secrets Of The Other Woman
Graham Masterton

"Night after night, all over the nation, couples are lying next to each other, needing each other, wanting each other, yet unable to communicate their desire by word or by gesture. A greater tragedy of noncommunication happens every night in this nation's marriage beds than all the years of the Cold War put together."

"It's impossible to say by how much the divorce rate could be reduced by better sexual communication. But there is no question that millions of potentially happy marriages are marred forever by nothing more dramatic than the inability of husbands and wives to discuss their sexual needs together." © 1

Do you find it difficult to talk about your sexual needs?

The Total Woman
Marabel Morgan

"Columnist Ann Landers discovered from a prominent divorce lawyer that nine out of ten divorces start in the bedroom. When a marriage goes on the rocks, the rocks are usually in the mattress. If a couple has a really good sexual relationship, they will try a lot harder to work out their problems and stay married."[2]

Would an unsatisfying sex life without hope of improvement cause you to dissolve a relationship? How long could you go without sexual intercourse and still preserve a healthy relationship?

How To Make Love All The Time
Barbara DeAngelis, Ph.D.

Secret One:

"Sex is very important to men to make them feel wanted. Men take sexual rejection very badly. They feel a woman is saying, 'I don't want you, I don't love you.' Since they don't always know how to express their hurt, they may retaliate by turning off to you, or seeking sex elsewhere.

So if you aren't in the mood for sex with your lover, say no to sex, but yes to loving him. (And men, you should do the same for women.)"©3

What are three, original, creative ways to lovingly say, "I'm not in the mood."?
What T.V. series or movie best describes your sex life?

More Ways To Drive Your Man Wild In Bed
Graham Masterton

"I want a friend, I want a wife, I want a lover, I want a whore, I want a princess, I want a critic, I want a business partner, I want a hostess. I want a mother for my children; I want someone who makes me laugh, someone who understands me when I'm down, someone who forgives me when I'm unjust, and stands up to me when I'm angry. I want someone who can walk into a room beside me and make me feel like I'm royalty. I want someone who can talk dirty and really turn me on. I want someone whose lips can speak words of warmth, words of reason, and words of judgement, yet will use those same lips to kiss my penis." © 4

What do *you* want in a woman?

Super Marital Sex
Paul Pearsall, Ph.D.

"Super Marital Sex Rule: Your parents' marriage affects your own style of being married,but it must be a starting point, not a goal to be achieved or an end to be avoided."©5

In what ways have your parents' behavior and attitude toward sex influenced or affected your sexuality?

The Art of Kissing
William Kane

"Recent sex surveys indicate that modern lovers believe kissing is one of the most essential aspects of a relationship, yet men and women are increasingly reporting that there is not enough kissing in their love lives." ©6

Why don't men and women kiss each other more often?

Light Her Fire
Ellen Kreidman

"Sex for her is kindness, gentleness, devotion, commitment, caring, patience, and compliments. It starts in the morning with whether you said "I love you" before you left. It's telling her how much she means to you. It's going shopping with her. It's helping her with chores. It's noticing that she has a new dress or hairdo. It's asking her to dinner. It's whether you phoned to say you'll be late. It's bringing home a card or a gift. Real romance for a woman is letting her know she's special, appreciated and loved. It's you spending time reaching out to her in a very giving way."

"Unlike most men, a woman will not be in the mood to make love just because you are there. She'll be in the mood because you are nice to her." ©7

What does sex mean to you?

How To Make Love All The Time
Barbara DeAngelis, Ph.D.

"Secret Three: Men like women who like sex."

"Don't let the men do all the work, ladies. Show them you want them; tell them how much you love sex. Take a risk, and you will find you are feeling sexier, too!" ©3

Would you like your lady to pursue you sexually more often? What percent of the time would you like her to make the sexual advances?

The Intimate Male
Linda Levine, ACSW and Lonnie Barbach, Ph.D.

"What makes for good sex?"

The overwhelming majority of men felt their emotional attachment to the woman they were making love to made the critical difference. Men described the importance of having relationships in which there were love, gentleness, caring and warmth. Although the physical aspect of lovemaking was important, it was mainly seen as a vehicle for expressing love and caring." © 9

For sex to be really good, what elements must be present?

The Art of Kissing
William Cane

"Kissing should stand alone as a sensual pleasure that deserves to be enjoyed for itself without going on to other sex acts. Kissing can bring two people closer than——because it's a more personal interaction. Which is why many prostitutes won't kiss their customers. They'll——for hours but won't kiss because kissing is considered even more intimate than——."

How could a little time devoted daily to the art of kissing improve your level of intimacy?

Why Men Are The Way They Are
Warren Farrell, Ph.D.

"Men who hop from one beautiful woman to another are usually looking for what they could not find at the last hop: good communication, shared values, good chemistry."[10]

What compromises may be necessary for two people to achieve sexual harmony?

The Art of Sexual Ecstasy
Margo Anand

"Many people have been deprived in their childhood of the nourishment that comes through being touched, held, and cuddled. Research has shown that this deprivation can cause emotional disturbances such as depression, hyperactivity, and aggression. Because cuddling is often considered a prelude to lovemaking rather than a tender activity in itself, there is a tendency for some people-women especially-to engage in sex when their real desire is only to be held and caressed."[©12]

Would you be willing to just cuddle X amount of nights in the week if you knew that the nights you did have sex, she would be even more loving and eager to please you?

Is There Sex After Marriage?
Carol Botwin

"One subject that couples rarely discuss is frequency of sex. Various studies have shown that dissatisfaction with sexual frequency is often a silent problem in marriage: one partner may want more sex, the other less, but neither is willing to talk about it. Experts find that mutually acceptable compromises can often be worked out—three times a week instead of five, or twice a week instead of once, for example— but only if the matter is discussed." © 11

If one partner wants more sex than the other, how do you work it out?

Sex Begins In The Kitchen

Dr. Kevin Leman

"Men think that sex, sexual intercourse, is the most special physical act. But women will say the most special physical act is holding, just physical holding.

"To correct or offset problems in a relationship, the couple has to learn the skill of being close without having sexual intercourse. There need to be times when they can just cuddle up and be close, hold each other's hands, scratch each other's backs, rub each other's feet be close, loving, caring-but no sex. Men like to be held too!"©13

On "just cuddling" nights, what forms of affection do you like? What one substitute would you choose as an occasional alternative to sex?

How to Make Love Six Nights A Week
Graham Masterton

"Having frequent sex does very much more than release tensions. It raises your self-esteem; it re-establishes your closeness with your partner; it defines your status as a woman; it demonstrates that somebody needs you and desires you . . . not just every now and then . . . but all the time." (pg. 52)

"Frequent sex is good for your self-confidence. Frequent sex is good for your physical fitness and general well-being. Frequent sex gives you a more positive and creative attitude toward life and will have a direct beneficial effect on anything that you're trying to achieve, either at home or at work. Frequent sex makes you more calmer and less irritable . . . Frequent sex improves your self-image. Frequent sex helps you to explore the full potential of your emotions, your body, and your imagination. Without any exaggeration, frequent sex can change your life from top to bottom."©40 (pgs. 62-63)

For you, how often does sex have to be to be frequent?

How To Put Love Back Into Making Love
Dagmar O'Connor

"The shame of masturbation runs deep in most of us. Rare indeed is the person who did not masturbate under a cloud of disgrace. Most couples experience a rush of relief just by "confessing" their secret. Without full realizing it, they have each been carrying a load of guilt around with them. The confession—often a mutual confession—begins to mitigate that guilt immediately. And the next step, of actually demonstrating your secret to one another, usually sets free the rest of that guilt."[15]

While growing up, did you feel guilty, secretive or embarrassed about masturbation? How do you feel about it now?

For Yourself
Lonnie Garfield Barbach, Ph.D.

"Masturbation is one of the best ways to learn about your sexual responses. Once you learn about how you respond—through stimulating yourself while free of outside distractions—you will be in a better position to shift your own body movement during love-making to achieve more pleasure or to teach your partner how to stimulate you in the manner that is most likely to lead you to sexual pleasure and eventually to orgasm." © 14

Was your first orgasm intentional or accidental?

The Hite Report on Male Sexuality
Shere Hite

"Do most men masturbate?

"When asked, 'How often do you masturbate?' almost all men, whether married or single, with or without an otherwise active sex life, said they made masturbation a regular part of their lives."[©16]

What sensations do you feel from self-stimulation that you don't experience with your lover?

The Hite Report on Female Sexuality
Shere Hite

"Masturbation is, in a very real sense, one of the most important subjects discussed in this book and a cause for celebration, because it is such an easy source of orgasms for most women. Women in this study said that they could masturbate and orgasm with ease in just a few minutes." © 17

How would it affect you to learn that the woman in your life masturbates?

Men In Love
Nancy Friday

"Watching a woman masturbate is one of the greatest of all masculine turn-ons. By breaking the rules, the woman has joined the man in expressing unfettered desire. The gap between love and lust has been bridged, the conflict resolved, and only excitement is left."[18]

What effect would, or does, watching your lover stimulate herself have on you? Would it excite you and lead to more fulfilling lovemaking?

How To Put The Love Back Into Making Love
Dagmar O'Connor

"I want you to masturbate simultaneously in front of each other—what I call 'tandem masturbation.' I know this may sound like just the opposite of intimacy, but believe me, once you dare to break through this barrier, once you share your ultimate secret with each other, you have a chance to experience an intimacy so profound that every aspect of your relationship will be enriched by it forever."[©15]

How could tandem self-stimulation in front of each other be informative in learning a partner's sexual response? Do you think this might create an even stronger intimacy?

Sex and Human Loving
Masters and Johnson

"Not everyone shares the same sexual tastes and preferences. If your partner won't participate in some form of sex that you find quite appealing, the important thing to remember is that he or she is rejecting the activity, not rejecting you. Try to talk out the problem without using an accusatory tone, since it may be possible to find some compromise solution."[20]

What sexual activities, if any, do you find unappealing or objectionable?

Nice Girls Do
Dr. Irene Kassorla

"Contrary to popular belief, increased sensuality offers increased safety to a relationship. As a woman becomes more sensual, she will feel more confident with herself and safer in the relationship.

"Many scientific studies have found that women who are sensual and orgasm more frequently, tend also to be more successful, more motivated in their work, and are more able to express feelings of hightened self-worth and self-esteem."[19]

Many women hold back their sexuality because they think it is not lady like or fear they may be perceived as promiscuous, the good girl/bad girl image. What would you say to the woman in your life to assure her that she could be as sexually uninhibited as she wants with you?

**His Needs,
Her Needs**
Willard F. Harley, Jr.

"In most couples I see in counseling, the woman craves affection. I try to help the man see that for a woman, affection has meaning far beyond anything he can imagine. A woman experiences immeasurable pleasure from the sensations she receives through affection. Although these sensations are not the same ones she enjoys during sexual arousal and intercourse, they form a vital part of the relationship, because without them she usually cannot get the most from a sexual experience."[21]

Do you feel that daily expressions and demonstrations of affection contribute to good sex or do you expect a woman to respond sexually without affection?

Why Men Don't Get Enough Sex and Women Don't Get Enough Love
Jonathan Kramer, Ph.D./Diane Dunaway

"Be a mistress, flirt with him, keep him interested. Men become sexually bored more easily than women do, and they are not supposed to seek variety outside of the relationship, though many do, of course. The secret is to keep variety within the relationship.

"Everything gets stale if it's repeated the same way over and over. Experiment. Try making love in different rooms, in different positions, with different music, with candles, with sexy videos or movies beforehand. Prepare for the encounter: go out to dinner, wear a very sexy outfit, and tease him during the evening by telling him what you're going to do to him later. Get yourself excited and get comfortable being sexual with your man. Shower or bathe together. Wear something sexy to bed. Turn down the lights."©[41]

When does foreplay begin and how important is it to you?

Sex and Human Loving

Masters and Johnson

"One of the most common complaints we have heard from men is that their female partners don't hold the penis firmly enough once it is erect. It may be surprising, but relatively few heterosexual men and women have taken the time to show their partners how they like to have their genitals touched.

A hands-on demonstration is often the simplest way of conveying an accurate message."[20]

It takes curiosity, patience, and desire to learn mutually rewarding manual stimulation. Are you willing to open up and show your lover exactly how you like to be touched? How would you teach this?

The Joy of Sex
Alex Comfort, M.D.

"Sex for all males and females begins in the handwork class-both when we start to discover our own bodies and when we start to have access to each other's. For both sexes it is basic training-in mutual sex good handwork is never superseded. A couple who can masturbate each other really skillfully can do anything else they like. Handwork is not a 'substitute' for vaginal intercourse but something quite different, giving a different type of orgasm, and the orgasm one produces oneself is different again from orgasm induced by a partner."[24]

Do you feel that manual stimulation to orgasm, induced by your lover, would add welcome variety to your total sex life? How often would you want to include this in your lovemaking?

Right-Brain Sex
Carol G. Wells

"Another important consideration for women who have orgasm problems has to do with receiving effective stimulation. As you remember, the orgasm reflex is triggered by a buildup of erotic stimulation. Some women need more time for this buildup than other women and, generally, more buildup time than men. Not surprisingly, then, some women never receive either enough stimulation or the right kind of stimulation to build up to orgasm. Losing control to sensations won't produce orgasms if the sensations are either not pleasurable or don'tlast long enough to move through the plateau phase to the orgasm phase."©46

How long does it usually take you to reach orgasm through self-stimulation, manual stimulation by a partner, oral sex, and intercourse?

What Turns Men On
Brigitte Nioche

"Why aren't women aware of the power they have over men?

"If you doubt that we have power, just think of the men you know who worship their wives or lovers. Have you ever asked yourself why he adores her? Or did you think that she was just lucky to find such a loving man? In most cases luck doesn't have much to do with it. What you are looking at is a sexually satisfied man whose woman knows how to please him. She uses her sexual powers to bewitch him. ©42

Who has the most power over you sexually:
a woman who reminds you of the Happy Hooker,
a Playboy centerfold or a Miss America?

The Sensuous Couple
Robert Chartham

"Scientifically speaking-and I'm not joking-the ideal time for a session is between 6 a.m. and 8 a.m. It has been discovered that most men's daily production cycle of testosterone-the hormone that-among other things makes him feel sexually responsive-is at its peak at 7 a.m. The Sensuous Couple, however, will vary the time, as they do the place, to get variety into their love lives and so avoid an encounter with that vicious love killer, boredom."[23]

What is your favorite and least favorite time of day to make love? How about to the nearest minute?

Light Her Fire

Ellen Kreidman

"When you start your lovemaking it is important that you don't begin by stroking her intimate parts. You want to prepare her for this enjoyment later. Kissing, hugging, and cuddling are essential for her to become aroused. Stroking and being stroked is an exciting activity you both can enjoy. Don't cheat yourself out of the warmth and stimulation that touching each other produces." ©7

Do you know the kinds of foreplay your lover enjoys and how much she needs?

Why Men Don't Get Enough Sex And Women Don't Get Enough Love
Jonathan Kramer, Ph.D. / Diane Dunaway

"The clitoris is a powerful center of sexual arousal that, in fact, serves no other purpose. It is a highly sensitive organ with a tremendous number of nerve endings, making it highly sensitive to touch. The majority of women need clitoral or other nonvaginal stimulation to reach orgasm, and most women need continual stimulation to achieve orgasm. If stimulation ceases, the woman's progress toward climax ceases. "Orgasm is easiest for most women to achieve through clitoral stimulation, though many women feel that the orgasm is preferable if they are penetrated at the same time. Most women climax through penetration and clitoral stimulation together, and few women achieve through penetration alone."[41]

How would it make you feel if your lover could not reach orgasm during intercourse without some form of manual stimulation?

His Needs, Her Needs

Willard F. Harley, Jr.

"The First Thing He Can't Do Without—Sexual Fulfillment.

A man cannot achieve fulfillment in his marriage unless his wife is sexually fulfilled as well. While I have maintained that men need sex more than women, unless a woman joins her husband in the sexual experience, his need for sex remains unmet. Therefore, a woman does her husband no favors by sacrificing her body to his sexual advances. He can feel sexually satisfied only when she joins him in the experience of lovemaking."©[21]

Does an occasional "quickie" at unexpected times and places fulfill a special sexual need for you? What is your definition of a "quickie" and how long does it last?

**Secrets About Men Every Woman
Should Know**
Barbara DeAngelis, Ph.D.

"Talk with your partner about having sex and making love. You may find, as hundreds of women I've advised have, that your man has been hesitant to express his purely sexual desires to you for fear of turning you off or offending you, or having you misinterpret his lust as being a sign that he doesn't love you. Ask him if he ever does a rush job seducing you because he really isn't in the mood. That may explain what you may have thought was his insensitivity or lack of expertise." © 32

What is the difference between having sex and making love?

Right-Brain Sex
Carol G. Wells

"Because passionate sex is a right-brain activity and because most of us tend to operate much too often in the left-brain, we easily get into trouble with our sexuality. When we allow our sexual activity to become too routine, we switch to our left-brain. Eventually we will become bored. At this point we will find ourselves either losing interest in our partner or in sex."[©46]

When you go home tonight, if you initiated a Right-brain sexual encounter and in the morning a Left-brain sexual encounter, how would they differ? Which side usually controls your lovemaking?

The New Joy of Sex
Alex Comfort, M.D.

"Women have the keener sense of smell, but men respond to it more as an attractant. In lovemaking, the note changes in regular order, from the totality of skin and gousset to her 'excited' note, then to her full genital odor, then, when intercourse has begun, to a different scent."[45]

What is the aroma of passion?

Lose Weight Through Great Sex With Celebrities! (the Elvis way)
Colin McEnroc

"In the book, "How to Find a Husband in 30 Days," author Wendy Stehling says you should wear erotic underwear. Stehling is very big on wild underthings and even takes the position that "all woman look good in garter belts." I've found that this whole subject is a great way to get into unpleasant arguments with women. Anyway, you can go too far with this underwear stuff. Something black and a little lacy is just great. Something with a battery-powered windmill blade is probably overreaching." © 28

Name three objects that, when looked at, arouse erotic desire in you?

Tantric Sex
E.J. Gold and Cybele Gold

"During the course of your ordinary sex, break contact before either of you is able to have an orgasm."

"Immediately withdraw physical contact, quietly get dressed, and do something else together. Anything but sex." © 30

Do you believe that stopping intercourse just short of orgasm can build anticipation that will lead to a more exciting orgasm at a later time?

How to Make Love Six Nights a Week
Graham Masterton

"I have had scores of letters from women who have been married for years and years, and have never experienced a 'real' climax (although they dare not tell their partners).

One of the key secrets to having frequent and satisfying sex is to make sure that you do have regular climaxes...real climaxes, and that your lover is not only aware that you need them but knows how to give them to you, too."[40]

Would you want your lover to confide that she had been "faking it" so you could try to help her achieve a real orgasm through the knowledge gained from this book?

The One Hour Orgasm
Bob Schwartz, Ph.D.

"There is only one answer to having a really successful relationship with a man. You, as women, need to be willing to train us and tell us the truth."©31

If you saw the movie, "When Harry Met Sally," you know a woman can "fake it." Do you want to know *every time* you make love whether she is really satisfied or will you be just as happy to let her pretend some of the time?

How To Make Love To Each Other
Alexandra Penny

"Genital kissing, as well as kissing of every other part of the body, is a sensual experience that is meant to give pleasure and warmth to the recipient. Fears of body odors are one of the deterrents to genital kissing. Sex therapists underscore that the natural scents of clean genitals are usually attractants to the opposite sex and that scented bathing or showering can, if desired, be incorporated into lovemaking itself."[8]

For oral sex to be really desirable, do you like your lover to be freshly bathed, natural, earthy or does it matter?

The One Hour Orgasm

Bob Schwartz, Ph.D.

"One of the most difficult things for a woman to ask of her man is to be pleasured sexually."

"Our job as men is to keep our women happy. Why? Because there is nothing more beautiful in the whole world than a turned-on and happy woman."[31]

What do you enjoy most about kissing a woman's body?

How To Put The Love Back Into Making Love

Dagmar O'Connor

"What I really want you to do is to bring sensuality into all of your life. Sensuality has a wonderful way a trickling from one part of your life to another. I have always maintained that if you learned how to eat sensually—to chew languorously, to run your tongue around the inside of your mouth, to smack your lips, to savor the texture of each morsel and the subtleties of each spice—you would automatically begin to make love more sensuously. And vice versa." © 15

Do you think there might be a connection between how you eat food and how you make love?

The Joy of Sex
Alex Comfort, M.D.

"Our own experience is that mutual genital kisses are wonderful, but if you are going to orgasm it's usually better to take turns." © 24

Do you think giving and receiving genital kisses should be about 50-50, or do you think one lover should give more than the other?

Why Men Don't Get Enough Sex and Women Don't Get Enough Love

Jonathan Kramer, Ph.D. / Diane Dunaway

"Some men like the naughty girl image of black and red or leather. Others prefer the sweet girl-next-door image. Decide what he will like best or vary your images. Remember not to be predictable. Do something he does not expect. Do something daring, even slightly dangerous or forbidden. He may not entirely approve, but it will probably excite him anyway.

Besides, men don't leave women for being sexy, unpredictable, and slightly dangerous. They leave them for being boring."[©41]

Should oral sex be included every time you make love or should it be unpredictable?

How To Make Love Six Nights a Week
Graham Masterton

"The trouble is, sexual problems are always more difficult to solve than any other kind of personal problems because they're so intimate and because they're all tangled up with embarrassment and pride. Every man likes to believe that he's the best lover in the world, and few women have the nerve to tell them that they're not. Similarly, just as few men have the nerve to tell the women in their lives that their lovemaking is awkward and unresponsive."[©40]

What is "bad sex"?
How do you spell great sex?

168

Secrets About Men Every Woman Should Know
Barbara DeAngelis, Ph.D.

Secret 5

"Men love receiving oral sex from a woman. The essence of loving your partner orally has to do with loving and adoring his most vulnerable part. Sure, it feels fantastic to your partner. But more than that, it makes him feel received and accepted." © 32

What feelings do you get from oral sex that you don't feel with intercourse?

Why Men Stray And Why Men Stay
Alexandra Penny

"One last word on technique: It's important to know physical technique for every part of lovemaking, but it's crucial to oral sex-and oral sex is number one on the majority of men's lists of what they love sexually. Most men are naturally highly reluctant to tell a woman that she's not doing "it" right; the woman who really knows how to satisfy a man is a technically skillful lover-and she knows exactly how to delight him with oral sex."[©48]

If your lover is not pleasing you orally, do you give her verbal guidance? What oral techniques do you like best?

Is There Sex After Marriage?
Carol Botwin

"Don't expect sex to be great everytime. Not every sexual experience can be fantastic. Even when two partners are sexually compatible, it is normal for sex sometimes to be good, sometimes so-so, sometimes disappointing—and, with luck, sometimes wonderful. Sexual appetites fluctuate as well. Our hormone levels go up and down; our state of physical or mental well-being changes. These things, as well as events in our lives, can affect our libido. To expect your sex life always to operate at a peak level is to set yourself up for feeling disappointed when normal highs and lows occur." © 11

If you've had sex and it wasn't particularly satisfying, do you blame yourself or your partner?

Sex and Human Loving
Masters and Johnson

"Don't be trapped into thinking that sex has always got to include intercourse to be meaningful or gratifying. By occasionally omitting intercourse from a lovemaking session, you may even discover other pleasures that are equally arousing."[20]

Do you sometimes like to make love without it leading to sexual intercourse?

Right-Brain Sex
Carol G. Wells

"Boredom in relationships is probably the most extensive and serious challenge facing us. Our culture and family life is structured around monogamy. Monogamy, all too often, gets turned into monotony. The novelty factor in any relationship tends toward a decline the longer the relationship continues."[©46]

What do you think is the most frequent sexual complaint of couples?

Nice Girls Do
Dr. Irene Kassorla

"Silence isn't golden in bed."

"Silence during lovemaking breeds alienation, increases anxiety, and squelches performance. Talking promotes self-confidence, stimulates action, and encourages intimacy. Enjoy your precious sexual moments as you begin unlocking your tongue. Learn the language of real intimacy and sensuality. Learn the language of love."© [19]

During lovemaking, do you prefer love language, lusty language or both?

The Sensuous Man
By "M"

"Each kind of bed-talk has a different purpose and a distinctive style. You can be a more desirable sex partner just by learning when to talk and what to talk about in bed. And a happier human being as well, since the things you say in bed can be an important emotional release. In fact, for some men the release of words during intercourse is more important than the release of semen."[26]

If your lady assured you that you could talk as naughty as you like when the two of you are making love, do you think you could really let go? What would you say to her that you haven't?

My Secret Garden
Nancy Friday

"I suggest that the next time you see that pretty female face with the Mona Lisa smile you consider, just consider, that she may not be thinking of a knight on a horse, just the horse."[©35]

Should lovers tell each other *all* their sexual fantasies? Do you feel guilty and disturbed about your sexual fantasies or do you try to accept them as normal?

Women On Top
Nancy Friday

I have always believed that our erotic daydreams are the true X rays of our sexual souls, and like our dreams at night they change as new people and situations enter our lives to be played out against the primitive backdrop of our childhood. An analyst collects his patients' dreams like gold coins. We should value our erotic reveries no less seriously, because they are the complex expressions of what we consciously desire and unconsciously fear. To know them is to know ourselves better.©47

Do you think you could accept any sexual fantasy your lover might reveal to you? If not, what types of fantasies might make you feel threatened or suspicious?

Sex Secrets of The Other Woman
Graham Masterton

"If you can discover the "trigger" fantasy that
stimulates your man, you can have tremendous
control over his sexual arousal. You can
enhance his physical excitement by joining in
his fantasy, embellishing it, becoming part of it.
What you can do, in fact, is to make yourself
indistinguishable from his most powerful sexual thoughts." © 1

What is the one fantasy, the *trigger* fantasy, that
you think about most?

Light His Fire
Ellen Kreidman

" 'X' marks the spot. Make reservations at an X-rated motel. Give yourself permission to be wicked."[27]

If you could go to a fantasy hotel, what love games would you play?

More Ways To Drive Your Man Wild In Bed
Graham Masterton

"I asked fifty different men from different backgrounds what their greatest sexual fear was and apart from an understandable percentage who were worried that they would not be able to get and keep an erection when they were in bed with a woman whom they wanted to impress, the largest proportion of them admitted that they were anxious about not being able to satisfy their women." [4]

How important is your woman's orgasm to you?

Shared Intimacies

Lonnie Barbach, Ph.D. and Linda Levine, A.C.S.W.

"Women favor certain intercourse position because they provide more clitoral stimulation than others. The amount of clitoral stimulation seems to be determined by the anatomical fit of the woman and her partner. Those positions which allow for direct stimulation of the clitoris by their partners pubic bone or which provide sufficient space for manual stimulation were often preferred."[©25]

From what sexual positions do you get the most stimulation? Which would be your absolute favorite, if you had to choose one?

The Hite Report On Female Sexuality
Shere Hite

"Can a woman stimulate herself manually while she is with a man? In the same way that men said that women often don't give them the correct manual stimulation of their penis, isn't it difficult for one person to know just how to stimulate another? Although learning to do just that with a partner can be very loving and exciting, it is also very important for men and women to feel that they can stimulate themselves during sex with a partner. This can be an extremely intimate activity, while at the same time removing many frustrations and pressures from both the woman and the man."©17

How does, or would, it make you feel if your lover manually stimulates herself while you are making love to her?

Why Men Stray And Why Men Stay
Alexandra Penny

"If I asked you, "Quick! Name the three things your lover likes most when you make love," you should be able to answer that question as fast as you can recite your ABC's, but the fact is that many women can't. Even though we may know exactly what our husbands desire for dinner, we aren't nearly as sure about what satisfies their appetites in bed. If you're not meeting his sexual needs, by now you should know just how much trouble that can lead to."©48

Quick, what are the three things your lover likes most when you make love?
Ditto for you . . .

Women on Top
Nancy Friday

"I hadn't yet learned that for women masturbation without fantasy is rare. It simply hadn't occurred to me that women could be more guilty about what they were thinking than what they were doing.

It is the mind that carries the genesis of sexual life, inhibits us from orgasm or releases us. Masturbation gets its fire, its life from what is sparked in the mind. The fingers might move across the clitoral region indefinitely without orgasm; only when the mind constructs the correct image, a scenario meaningful and powerful to us alone because it carries us up and past all fears of reprisals and into that forbidden interior world that is our own sexual psyche—only then do we come."[©47]

Do you use a visual image, or a sexual fantasy to reach orgasm through masturbation? Oral sex? Intercourse?

The Sensuous Woman
By "J"

"When you have educated your body to the point where it can reel off several orgasms at your command, you will be able to guide him, when you are making love to positions that give you the maximum sensation. After all, if *you* don't know what sets your body off sensually, how can you can expect *him* to know? Every woman is different and he's not clairvoyant." © 36

Who's responsible for the female orgasm?

How To Make Love To A Man
Alexandra Penny

"You have far more control of your mouth and your hands than you do of your vagina. Your mouth and hands can give your partner a variety of exquisite sensations that can repeatedly bring him to the brink of climax." © 29

What is the difference between an oral orgasm and orgasm from intercourse?

Total Loving
by "J"

"Silent sex is, if you think about it, rather insulting. If he invited you out to a gourmet dinner, you wouldn't plow through the whole feast without telling him how delicious each course was." © 38

Are silent orgasms as exciting as verbal orgasms?

How To Drive Your Man Wild In Bed
Graham Masterton

"When you actually have your orgasm, tell him what it's like. Some men seem to believe that it's nothing more than a quiet muscular wince, while others expect the Fourth of July to come bursting out of your ears. Good sex is always founded on good communication between lovers, and if he knows what your orgasm feels like, then he can identify more with your experience when he's making love to you."[22]

Before you climax, *how* do you make sure your lover has been satisfied?

The Sensuous Man
by "J"

"The responsibility of the man to carry the burden of sexual success would be no great concern if we didn't place a high value on that success. But we do. Every young boy is taught that a man is supposed to be 'masculine'. And, as he becomes a teen-ager, he learns, through gossip, reading, and the media, that every real man is expected to be a good sexual performer."[©26]

What sexual insecurities do you have?

Light His Fire
Ellen Kreidman

"Play Ball."
"If he played football in school, make love to him on the football field. If he played soccer, make love to him on the soccer field, and if he played basketball, make love to him in the gym. If he was a spectator, make love to him under the bleachers!" © 27

Do you enjoy sex-in-danger-of-being-caught-situations?

How To Make Love To A Man
Alexandra Penny

"The more stimulation that a man experiences, the more intense and dramatic his orgasm will be. The sexually knowledgeable woman will physically prolong a man's erection so that he (as well as she) can experience an orgasm in its ultimate intensity."[29]

How many times do you like to be brought to the brink of orgasm before it actually happens?

What Men Won't Tell You But Women Need To Know
Bob Berkowitz

"And this may come as a surprise, but many times we do not know when you have an orgasm. Some women, of course, scream and yell and make it sound like Mount Vesuvius erupting, and men aren't so numb that they don't know what that means.

"But, believe me, there are some women who do not convey the same unmistakable message to a man. I'm not suggesting that you start whooping it up and screeching, 'Touchdown!' every time you have an orgasm. Just under-stand that many men are unable to break the code. We don't know for sure."[43]

Some men do not know *for sure* when a woman is having an orgasm. Would you like her to tell you, with words, when she is climaxing so you could enjoy the experience with her?

Sex and Human Loving
Masters and Johnson

"During orgasm, penile stimulation is variable: some men slow down, others hold the penis firmly, and others stop all stimulation."[©20]

To increase the intensity of your orgasm during intercourse or oral sex, when you start to climax, do you want her to speed up, slow down or stop all stimulation?

The Sensuous Woman
By "J"

"The smart woman never forgets the importance or arousing him mentally. Whispering to him exactly what you intend to do to him in bed will create pictures in his mind that are likely to excite him almost as much as the actuality."©₃₆

If a woman wanted to intensify your orgasm, what words should she whisper in your ear right before?

The Sensuous Man
By "M"

"The sighs and groans of ecstasy have faded away. You lie in bed in your woman's arms. What fulfillment! What contentment! And, if you're like me, you're falling asleep, WAKE UP! Keep touching, fondling, and caressing her; don't roll over and turn away from your partner as if you were finished with her. Your touch now is more precious than ever. This is the time for closeness.

It is also the time for communication. Probably no other occasion is more suited for real communication than the moments following intercourse."[26]

When you are basking in the afterglow of making love, what is the first thing you want to hear?

Mind
Questions

There is a woman at the beginning of
all great things.

Alphonse de Lamartine

What is the greatest gift you have to offer a woman?

Personality is the sum total of all the feelings in any conscious life up to its present moment.

Alexander Bain

How many personalities do you have?
How many voices?

I think, therefore I am.

Rene Descartes

Using five adjectives, how would you describe
yourself?

The mother's heart is in the child's school room.

Henry Word Beecher

What did you learn from your mother?

Without knowing the force of words it is
impossible to know men.

Albert Einstein

Under what circumstances, if any, could you
forgive infidelity and continue the relationship?

No man really becomes a fool until he stops
asking questions.

Charles Proteus Steinmitz

Is there a chance you could have contracted AIDS
by a blood transfusion, through a homosexual or
heterosexual relationship? Have you been tested
for HIV? What form of protection do you use?

A woman is more considerate in affairs of love
than a man, because love is more the study and
business of her life.

Washington Irving

In a recent survey, 100,000 men were
asked, "Have you ever had an extramarital
affair?" Seventy-eight percent replied, "Yes."

Why do you think most men are not
monogamous?

It's awfully hard for a woman to pretend not to know the things she ought to know.

Robert Chambers Edwards

What type of woman turns you off emotionally and sexually? Is there a difference?

My greatest inspiration is a challenge to attempt
the impossible.

Albert Abraham Michelson

How can one lover satisfy all your sexual needs
for the rest of your life?

To abandon the struggle for private happiness,
to expel all eagerness of temporary desire,
to burn with passion for external things – this is
emancipation, and this is the free man's worship.

Bertrand Russell

What do you consider to be the seven greatest
things in life?

Forgiveness is the fragrance of the violet which still clings fast to the heel that crushed it.

Unknown

When someone you care about hurts you, how do you forgive and forget?

I not only use all the brains I have, but all
I can borrow.

(Thomas) Woodrow Wilson

Past or present, what five people would you like
to borrow some brains from?

It doesn't matter what we know as long as we
know the same things.

George Santayana

How do you keep from being taken for granted?

Knowledge is Power.

Francis Bacon

What is the best way to end an argument?

The only way to have a friend is to be one.

Ralph Waldo Emerson

What is a friend?

Friendship is one mind in two bodies.

Mencius

Do you ever tell your friends how much you care about them?

Keep your heart free from hate. Expect little,
give much. Fill your life with love. Scatter
sunshine. Forget self, think of others.
Do as you would be done by.

Norman Vincent Peale

What golden rule do you *try* to live by?

Every house where love abides and friendship is
a guest, is surely home and home, sweet home;
for there the heart can rest.

Henry Van Dyke

What does your home mean to you?

A foe to God was never a true friend to man.

Edward Young

What is God?

Nearness to nature keeps the spirit sensitive to impressions not commonly felt, and in touch with unseen powers.

Ohiyesa

How do you keep in touch with mother nature?

Deliver me, O Lord, from that evil man, myself.

Thomas Brooks

How would you describe your dark side?

The life which is unexamined is not worth living.

Plato

In anger, do you tend to attack physically, verbally or both?

To me the pleasure of knowing is so great, so wonderful nothing has meant so much to me in all my life, as certain knowledge. Yes, it is the greatest thing in life-to know. It is really to be happy, to be free.

David Herbert Lawerence

What are the major factors in a lasting relationship?

The art of being wise is the art of knowing what
to overlook.

William James

How often do you have to have things your way
with little or no compromise? What will you not
compromise on?

Let all your views in life be directed to a solid, however moderate, independence; without it no man can be happy, nor even honest.

Junius

In a committed relationship, how much independence do you need?

The good man is the man who, no matter how morally unworthy he has been, is moving to become better.

John Dewey

In what two ways could you better yourself?

The sale doesn't begin until they say no.

Mike Curry

How many noes does it take before you believe it?

A woman who is not interested in sex must take the responsibility for an unfaithful man.

Brigette Nioche

Always treat a woman with respect and make her feel that she is the most beautiful woman in the world.

Laura Corn

If you were going to give someone a few years younger than yourself sexual advice, what would it be? Would the person's gender make a difference in your advice?

What do we live for, if it is not to make life less
difficult to each other.

George Eliot

What habits and idiosyncrasies do people have
that get on your nerves?

Know Thy Self.

Socrates

What is the meaning of your life?

Love is a prelude to life, the ultimate of one's existence.

George Santayana

How many people have you loved?

Great men are they who see that spiritual is stronger than any material force – that thoughts rule the world!

Ralph Waldo Emerson

What qualities do you admire in a man?

Look. This is your world! You can't not look.
There is no other world. This is your world; it is
your feast. You inherited this; you inherited
these eyeballs; you inherited this world of color.
Look at the greatness of the whole thing. Look!
Don't hesitate—look! open your eyes. Don't blink,
and look, look —look further.

Chögyam Trungpa

How do you see the world?

Angels fly because they take themselves lightly.

Unknown

If you wanted to give someone a good chuckle while walking by your tombstone, what would it say?

Not only are we ignorant of the true nature of the universe, for which we might be excused; we are also ignorant of the true nature of ourselves.

Henry David Thoreau

On the average what do you do more of: Listen or talk?

Life should always be lived with the feeling that
this may be one's last day on earth.

Eleanor Roosevelt

What bores you to tears?

Three passions, simple but overwhelmingly strong, have governed my life: the longing for love, the search for knowledge and the unbearable pity for the suffering of mankind.

Bertrand Russell

What do you feel *passionate* about?

We are very much what others think of us. The reception our observations meet with gives us courage to proceed, or dampens our efforts.

William Hazlitt

How do you think most people perceive you?

Every man ought to be inquisitive through every hour of his great adventure down to the day when he shall no longer cast a shadow in the sun. For if he dies without a question in his heart, what excuse is there for his continuance?

Frank Moore Colby

What questions do you have that you have not found the answers to?

Maturity means dependability, keeping one's word coming through in the crisis. The immature are masters of the alibi. They are the confused and disorganized. Their lives are a maze of broken promises, former friends, and good intentions that somehow never seem to materialize.

Ira G. Corn Jr.

When you give someone your word, do you stand behind it *one hundred percent?*

If you have knowledge, let others light their
candles at it!

Thomas Fuller

What have you learned in life?

Iris

The Iris is a flower and a golden winged goddess of the rainbow, carrying messages to men from God, traveling on the path of the rainbow.

Greek Mythology

How do you want to be remembered?

Mind's are conquered not by arms but by
greatness of soul.

Baurch Spinoza

How many people do you want at your funeral?

EDITORS NOTE:

The author is working on a sequel. If you feel your man has given a particularly romantic, sensuous or thoughtful answer to one or more questions, you are invited to submit them to:

Editor
Park Avenue Publishers
P.O. Box 20010
Oklahoma City, OK 73156

If used in the sequel, you will be given, with your permission, a credit line. Address and telephone number will be appreciated.

COPYRIGHT ACKNOWLEDGMENTS

Grateful acknowledgment for permission to quote song lyrics and publications in copyright is made to the following. Listing for songs is alphabetical by administrator, then song title.Publication copyright notices are footnoted to the text. Due to space constraint, recurring phrases are coded as follows: ARR=All Rights Reserved, CR= Copyright Renewed, ICS= International Copyright Secured, MUSA= Made in USA, RBP= Reprinted by Permission, UBP= Used by Permission.

Almo Music Corp/Irving Music Inc.

GOOD VIBRATIONS (BrianWilson) © 1966Irving Music,Inc(BMI) ARR,ICS
LADY IN RED (ChrisDeBurgh) © 1986 Rondor Music (London) Ltd (PRS) All Rts Adm in US & Canada by Almo Music Corp(ASCAP) ARR, ICS
LANGUAGE OF THE HEART (DavidWilcox) © 1989 Midnight Ocean Bonfire Music/Irving Music Inc. (BMI) All Rts Adm By Irving Music. ARR,ICS
POETRY MAN (Phoebe Snow) © 1973,1975 Almo Music Corp (ASCAP)ARR,ICS
THATS ENOUGH FOR ME (PaulWilliams) © 1970 Irving Music Inc ARR,ICS
WHEN SOMETHING IS WRONG WITH MY BABY (Isaac Hayes / David Porter) © 1966 Pronto Music/Irving Music Inc. (BMI) ARR,ICS

Bicycle Music Co.,

FOREVER IN BLUE JEANS(Neil Diamond / Richard Bennett)©1978 Stonebridge Music,ARR,UBP

Freddy Bienstock Enterprises

A LOVERS QUESTION(Brook Benton/Jimmy Williams)©1958 Alley Music Corp,Trio Music Co.Inc,Iza Music Corp., ARR, UBP
UNDER THE BOARDWALK(Arthur Resnick/Kenny Young)©1964 Alley Music Corp./Trio Music Co.,Inc., UBP, ARR

Big Sky Music

LAY,LADY,LAY(BobDylan)©1969 Big Sky Music, ARR, ICS, RBP

BMG Music Publishing

SAILING(Christopher Cross)©BMG Songs Inc.(ASCAP) ARR, UBP

Cherio Corporation

YOUNG AT HEART(Carolyn Leigh/Johnny Richards)© 1954 Cherio Corp. Renewed 1982 Cherio Corp and June's Tunes, ICS, ARR

Cherry Lane Music Publishing Inc.

ANNIE'S SONG(John Denver)©1974 Cherry Lane Music Publ. Co., Inc., ARR, UBP
AFTERNOON DELIGHT(Bill Danoff)©1975Cherry Lane Music Publ. Co., Inc., ARR, UBP

Chrysalis Music Group

SHE'S A LADY(Paul Anka)©1971 Management Agency & Music Publ.,Inc.
ICS, ARR, UBP

Cooper, Epstein & Hurewitz

DO THAT TO ME ONE MORE TIME(Toni Tennille)©1979 Moonlight &
Magnolias,Inc. (BMI)

CPP Belwin, Inc.

BLUE MOON(Richard Rodgers/Lorenz Hart)©1961 Metro-Goldyn
Mayer.Inc.,Adm by EMI-Robbins Catalog, ICS, MUSA, ARR
FOR THE GOOD TIMES(Kris Kristofferson)© 1968 Buckhorn Music
Publishers,Inc. ,UBP, MUSA, ARR.
I DON'T STAND A GHOST OF A CHANCE WITH YOU(Bing Crosby/
Ned Washington / Vincent Young)©1932 Mills Music,Inc.
IN A SENTIMENTAL MOOD(Duke Ellington/Irving Mills/Manny Kurtz)© 1935
American Academy of Music, Inc., CR 1963, ICS, MUSA, ARR.
INCURABLY ROMANTIC(Sammy Cahn/John Lane/James Van Heusen)
©1960,1988 Twentieth Century Music Corp., Adm. by EMI-Miller Catalog,Inc
LOVER(Lorenz Hart/Richard Rodgers)©1932,1933 Famous Music Corp,
CR1959,1960 Famous Music Corp, ICS, MUSA, ARR
MOCKINGBIRD (Inez Foxx/Charley Foxx/James Taylor)©1963,1974 Unart Music
Corp. All Rts Adm by EMI-Uniart Catalog, ICS, MUSA, ARR
MORE THAN YOU KNOW(Edward Eliscu/William Rose/Vincent Youmans)
©1929,1957 Miller Music Corp/Vincent Youmans,Adm by EMI Miller,
ICS, MUSA, ARR
NOBODY DOES IT BETTER(Carol Bayer Sager)© 1977 Danjaq S.A., Adm by
EMI Unart Catalog, ICS, MUSA, ARR
THE SWEETHEART TREE(Johnny Mercer/Henry Mancini)©1965 Northridge
Music Co.and Warner Bros.Music, ICS, MUSA, ARR
TRY A LITTLE TENDERNESS(Jimmy Campbell/Reg Connelly/Harry Woods)
©1932,1960 Campbell,Connelly & Co,Ltd., Adm. by EMI-Robbins Catalog
WEEKEND IN NEW ENGLAND(Marvin Hamlisch/Carol Bayer Sager) © 1975,
1976Unart Music Corp/ Piano Picker Music, Adm by EMI Unart Cata,ICS, ARR
YOU STEPPED OUT OF A DREAM (Gus Kahn/Nacio Herb Brown)©1940,1968
Leo Feist, Inc. All Rts Adm by EMI-Feist Catalog, ICS, MUSA, ARR

Donald Jay Music Ltd

I'VE HAD THE TIME OF MY LIFE(Frank Previte/Donald Markowitz/
John DeNicola)©1987 Knockout Music(ASCAP)/Donald Jay Music Ltd. (ASCAP)
/R.U.Cyrius Music(ASCAP)/Jemava Music Corp.(BMI)

Famous Music

HEART AND SOUL (Frank Loesser/Hoagy Carmichael)© 1938 Famous Music
Corp CR 1965 Famous Music Corp.
SPEAK SOFTLY LOVE(Larry Kusik/Nino Roto)©1972 Famous Music Corp.
TAKE MY BREATH AWAY(Giorgio Moroder / Tom Whitlock)©1986 Famous
Music Corp. and GMPC
THE NEARNESS OF YOU(Ned Washington/Hoagy Carmichael)©1937,1940
Famous Music Corp. . Copyright renewed 1964,1967 Famous Music Corp.

Bernie Fishback

OUR HOUSE(Graham Nash)©1970 Nash Notes, ARR

Frank Music Corp.

UNCHAINED MELODY(Hy Zaret/Alex North)©1955 Frank Music Corp.CR 1983 Frank Music Corp. ICS, ARR

Jerry Music Corp.

WITH YOU I'M BORN AGAIN(Carol Conners)© 1979 Checkout Music

Gelfand, Rennert & Feldman

I LOVE TO SEE YOU SMILE(Randy Newman)©1989 Twice As Nice Music and MCA Music Publ.

MCA Music Publishing

CRAZY HE CALLS ME(Bob Russell/Carl Sigman)©1949,1977 Harrison Music Corp./Major Songs, UBP, ICS, ARR

JAC Music Company, Inc

DON'T MAKE ME OVER(Hal David)©1962 JAC Music Co./Blue Seas Music, Renewed 1990 Casa David/New Hidden Valley Music
I SAY A LITTLE PRAYER(Hal David)©1966 Blue Seas Music/JAC Music Co.

Jobete Music Co.,Inc.

(LOVE IS LIKE A)HEAT WAVE(Edward Holland/Lamont Dozier/Brian Holland) ©1963 Stone Agate Music
HOW SWEET IT IS(TO BE LOVED BY YOU) (Edward Holland/Lamont Dozier/ Brian Holland)©1964 Stone Agate Music
I JUST CALLED TO SAY I LOVED YOU(Stevie Wonder)©1984 Jobete Music Co.,Inc./ Black Bull Music
SEND ONE YOUR LOVE(Stevie Wonder) © Jobete Music

June's Tunes

YOUNG AT HEART(Carolyn Leigh/Johnny Richards)©1954 Cherio Corp. Renewed 1982 Cherio Corp and June's Tunes, ICS, ARR

Le-Frak Moelis Records

I'LL HAVE TO SAY I LOVE YOU IN A SONG(Jim Croce)©1974,1985 Saja Music

Leiber & Stoller

I'M A WOMAN(Jerry Leiber/Mike Stoller)©1961(renewed) Jerry Leiber Music & Mike Stoller Music, ARR,, UBP
SIXTY MINUTE MAN(William Ward)©1951(renewed) Trio Music Co.,Inc. and Fort Knox Music. ARR, UBP

Floyd Leiberman

FEEL LIKE MAKING LOVE(Eugene McDaniels)©1974 Skyforest Music Co., Inc.

The Lowery Group

CHEVY VAN(Sammy Johns)©1976 Lowery Music Co.,Inc.Captain Crystal Music
Co.and Legibus Music Co., ICS, ARR, UBP

Maypop Music Group

FEELS SO RIGHT(Randy Owen)©1980 Maypop Music(a Div.of Wildcountry Inc.)
(YOU'VE GOT)THE TOUCH(Will Robinson/John Jarrad/Lisa Palas)© 1986
Alabama Band Music (a Division of Wildcountry Inc.)

Manett, Phelps, Rothenberg & Phillips

I SAY A LITTLE PRAYER(Hal David)©1966 Blue Seas Music,Inc,/JAC Music

MCA Music Publishing

I LOVE TO SEE YOU SMILE(Randy Newman)©1989 Twicw As Nice Music/ MCA
Music Publishing
LAUGHTER IN THE RAIN(Phil Cody/Neil Sedaka)©1974 Welback Music, Entco
Music and Suite 1510 Music,Rts of Welback Adm by MCA Music Publ. UBP,ARR
LOLLIPOPS AND ROSES(Tony Velona)©1960 Leeds Music Corp., Rts Adm
by MCA Music Publ., CR, UBP, ARR
SOMETIMES WHEN WE TOUCH(Dan Hill/Barry Mann)©1977 McCauley Music
Limited, ATV Music Corp. and Mann & Weil Songs, Inc., UBP, ARR
SUNDAY KIND OF LOVE(Barbara Belle/Louis Prima/Anita Leonard/Stan
Rhodes)©1964,1972 by MCA Music Publ., CR, UBP, ARR

Mitchell, Silberberg & Knupp

PICNIC(Steve Allen/George Duning)©1956 Columbia Pictures Music Corp.
Copyright Renewed 1984 by Steve Allen

Edwin H. Morris & Company

MISTER SANDMAN(Pat Ballard)©1954 Edwin H Morris & Co, a division of
MPL Communications Inc., ICS, ARR
SHE TOUCHED ME(Ira Levin/Milton Schafer)©1965 Ira Levin and Milton
Schafer All Rts Throughout World Controlled by Edwin H. Morris & Co.,ICS,ARR

MPL Communications Inc.

WILL WE EVER KNOW EACH OTHER(Martin Charnin/BobBrush)©1981,1982
MPL Communications Inc., ICS, ARR

Neil Music

CHERRY LIPS(Winfield Scott)© 1984 Neil Music, Inc.

Opryland Music Group

THERE'S A TEAR IN MY BEER(Hank Williams)©1952,1980 Acuff-Rose Music
Inc. and Hiriam Music. UBP, ARR, ICS
TILL I KISSED YOU(Don Everly)©1959,1987 Acuff-Rose Music Inc.(BMI)
UBP, ICS, ARR

The Clyde Otis Music Group

A LOVERS QUESTION(Brook Benton/Jimmy Williams)© 1974 Iza Music Corp./

George Pincus & Sons Music Corp

OLD CAPE COD(Claire Rothrock/Milt Yakus/Allan Jeffrey)©1956 George Pincus & Sons Music Corp. New York, NY, ICS, MUSA, AR

PolyGram/Island Music Publishing Group

A LOVELY WAY TO SPEND AN EVENING(Harold Adamson/Jimmy McHugh) ©1943 PolyGram International Publishing Inc.
ADDICTED TO LOVE(Robert Palmer)©1985 Bungalow Music N.V. worldwide, controlled by Akee Music, Inc.
CRACKERS(Rhonda Fleming/Dennis Morgan)©1980 Hall-Clements Publications, All Rights Administered by PolyGram International, Inc.
DON'T CRY(George Downes/John Wetton)©1983 Nosebag Music,Inc and Almond Legg Music Corp. All rts USA and Canada controlled by Island Music,Inc.
MAKE ME LOSE CONTROL(Dean Pitchford/Eric Carmen)©1988 Island Music, Inc and Eric Carmen Music
SMOKE GETS IN YOUR EYES(Otto Harbach/Jerome Kern)©1933 PolyGram International Publ., Inc.
THE WAY YOU LOOK TONIGHT(Jerome Kern/Dorothy Field)©1936 PolyGram International Publ.,Inc.

Quackenbush Music

ANTICIPATION(Carly Simon)©1971 Quackenbush Music,Ltd.
I LOVE TO SEE YOU SMILE(Randy Newman)© 1989 Twice as Nice Music & MCA Music Publ.

Terry Shaddick

PHYSICAL(Terry Shaddick)© 1981, Terry Shaddick Music

Shapiro, Bernstein & Co., Inc

PICNIC(Steve Allen/George Duning)©MCMLV,MCMLVI Columbia Pictures Music Corp. Copyright Renewed, Used By Permission.

Songwriters Guild of America

APRIL SHOWERS(B.G.DeSilva)©1929,1944 Steven Ballentine Publ.Co., Administered by SGA
CRAZY HE CALLS ME(Bob Russell/Carl Sigman)©1949,Renewed 1977 Harrison Music Corp./Major Songs, Administered by SGA, ICS, ARR.
HOW LOVELY TO BE A WOMAN(Lee Adams/Charles Strouse)©1960,1988 Strada Music All Rights Administered by SGA
MISTY(Johnny Burke/Earl Garner)©1955,1985,J.Burk Co.,s Rts Adm by SGA
WHEN YOUR HAIR HAS TURNED TO SILVER(Charlie Tobias/Pete DeRose) ©1930.1958, 1987 Carl Sigman/Major Songs. Administered by SGA

Sony Music Publishing

WOMAN(John Lennon)©1980 Leono Music, All Rts Adm by Sony Music Publ., Reprinted by Permission of the Publisher.

Warner/Chappell Music Inc.

ABRACADABRA(Steve Miller)©1982 Sailor Music, ARR, UBP

AFTER THE LOVIN(Ernesto Phillips)© 1989 Warner-Tamerlane Publ.
Corp., Eleksylum Music Inc.& Philesto Music,Inc.,Eleksylum and Philesto Rights
Administered by Warner-Tamerlane, UBP, ARR.

ALL SHOOK UP(Otis Blackwell/Elvis Presley)©1957 Unart Music Corp. All Rts
Adm by Unart Music Corp and Unichappell Music Inc., ARR, UBP.

ALL THE MAN THAT I NEED(Dean Pitchford/MichaelGore)©1982 Warner-
Tamerlane Publ. Corp, Body Electric Music and Fifth of March Music. All
Rts on behalf Body Electric Adm by Warner-Tamerlane,ARR, UBP.

ALWAYS ON MY MIND(Wayne Carson .Head/Johnny Christopher/Mark James)
©1971,1979 Screen-Gems Music,Inc.& Sebanine Music, Inc.All Rts Adm by Screen
Gems-EMI,ARR,UBP

BIG SPENDER(Cy Coleman/Dorothy Fields)©1965 Notable Music Co.,Inc. & Lida
Enterprises, Inc., All Rts Adm by WB Music Corp., ARR, UBP.

BEHIND CLOSED DOORS(Kenny O'Dell)©1973 Warner House of Music,
ARR, UBP

BOTH TO EACH OTHER(FRIENDS AND LOVERS)(Jay Gruska/Paul Gordon)
©1982,1986 Coldgems-EMI Music Inc.& French Surf Music, All Rts Adm by
Colgems-EMI Music, Inc and Warner Bros. Music Corp., ARR, UBP.

CHANCES ARE (Al Stillman/RobertAllen) © 1957(Renewed) Kitty-Ann Music Co.
Inc & Charlie Deitcher Productions, Inc., ARR, UBP.

CLOSE THE DOOR(Kenneth Gamble/Leon Huff)©1978 Warner-Tamerlane Publ.
Corp. ARR, UBP.

DON'T HOLD BACK YOUR LOVE(Richard Page/David Tyson/Gerald O'Brien)
©1990 WB Music Corp. Ali-Aja Music, David Tyson Music, EMI-Blackwood Music
&O'Brien Publ.. All Rts of Ali-Aja Music Adm by WB Music Corp.,ARR, UBP

GREAT BALLS OF FIRE(Otis Blackwell/Jack Hammer)©1957 Unichappell
Music,Inc. and Chappell & Co., ARR, UBP.

HOW DO YOU KEEP THE MUSIC PLAYING?(Michel Legrand/Alan and
Marilyn Bergman)©1982 WB Music Corp., ARR, UBP.

I ONLY HAVE EYES FOR YOU(Harry Warren/Al Dubin)©1934 Warner Bros.
Inc. CR All rights administered by Warner Bros, Inc. ARR, UBP

IN SEARCH OF THE PERFECT SHAMPOO(Michael Franks)©1978 Warner-
Tamerlane Publ. Corp., ARR, UBP.

IT HAD TO BE YOU(Isham Jones/Gus Kahn)©1924 Warner Bros. Inc.,
CR,ARR,UBP

IT'S THE STRANGEST THING(Fred Ebb/John Kandar)©1978 Unichappell Music
Inc & Kander-Ebb, Inc., ARR, UBP.

LET'S MISBEHAVE(Cole Porter)©1927 Warner Bros. Inc., CR, ARR, UBP.

MAKING LOVE(Burt Bacharach/Carol Bayer Sager/B Roberts)©1982 Warner-
Tamerlane Publ. Corp, WB Music Corp., New Hidden Valley Music,
Carole Bayer Sager Music and Boozertoones, Inc. ARR, UBP

MOONDANCE(Van Morrison)©1971 WB Music & Caledonia Soul Music, All Rts
Adm by WB Music Corp. ARR, UBP.

MY CUP RUNNETH OVER(Tom Jones/Harvey Schmidt)©1966 Tom Jones &
Harvey Schmidt All Rts Adm By Chappell & Co., ARR, UBP.

PEACEFUL EASY FEELING(Jack Tempchin)©1972 WB Music Corp. & Jazz Bird
Music All Rights Reserved, Used by Permission.

ROUND MIDNIGHT(Cootie Williams/Bernie Hanigan/Thelonius Monk)©1944
Warner Bros. Inc., CR. & Thelonius Monk Publ. Designee, ARR, UBP.

SLOW HAND(John Bettis/Michael Clark)©1981 Warner-Tamerlane Publ. Corp.,

Flying Dutchman Music & Sweet Harmony Music Inc., All Rts on behalf of Flying
Dutchman Adm By Warner-Tamerlane Publ. Corp., All Rts on behalf of Sweet
Harmony Music Adm by WB Music Corp.
THANK HEAVENS FOR LITTLE GIRLS(Alan Lerner/Frederick Loewe)
©1957,CR, Chappell & Co., ARR, UBP.
THE ROSE(Anita McBroom)©1979 Warner-Tamerlane Publ. Corp. and
Third Story Music Inc., ARR, UBP.
THE SECRET GARDEN(Quincy Jones/Siedah Garrett/Rod Temperton/El
Debarge)©1989,1990 He Bee Dooinit Music,Black Chick Music, WB Music
Corp.,Rodsongs, MCA Music Publ. and Rambush Music. ARR,UBP.
WHAT'S NEW?(Bob Haggart/Johnny Burke)©1939, CR,Warner Bros.,Inc.,
ARR, UBP.
WHEN DOVE'S CRY(Prince Nelson)©1984 Controversy Music, All Rts on behalf
of Controversy Music for USA & Canada Adm by WB Music Corp.,ARR,UBP
WHEN SOMETHING'S WRONG WITH MY BABY(IsaacHayes/David Porter)
©1966 Pronto Music/Irving Music, Inc., All Rts Adm By Warner-Tamerlane,
ARR, UBP
WISHIN' ON A STAR(Billy Calvin)©1977 Warner-Tamerlane Publ. Corp. &
May 12th Music,Inc., All Rts Adm by Warner Tamerlane, ARR, UBP.
YOU'D BE SO NICE TO COME HOME TO(Cole Porter)©1979 Chappell & Co.
ARR,UBP.
YOU GO TO MY HEAD(J. Fred Coots/Haven Gillespie)©1938 Warner Bros., Inc.,
CR. ARR, UBP.
YOU NEEDED ME(Randy Goodrum)©1975 Chappell & Co. and Ironside Music,
ARR,UBP.
YOU MAKE ME FEEL SO YOUNG(Josef Myrow/Mack Gordon)©1940 CR,
WB Music Corp. ARR,UBP
YOU SHOULD HEAR HOW SHE TALKS ABOUT YOU(Dean Pitchford/
Tom Snow) ©1981 Warner-Tamerlane Publ. Corp., Body Electric Music & Snow
Music, All Rts behalf of Body Electric Adm By Warner-Tamerlane, ARR, UBP.
YOU DO SOMETHIN TO ME(Cole Porter)©1929 Warner Bros. Inc.
CR. ARR, UBP.

Williamson Music

IF I LOVED YOU(Richard Rodgers/Oscar Hammerstein II)©1945 Williamson
Music Co.UBP, ARR
PEOPLE WILL SAY WE`RE IN LOVE(Richard Rodgers/Oscar Hammerstein II)
©1943 by Williamson Music Co. UBP, ARR
SOMETHING GOOD(Richard Rodgers)©1964 Richard Rodgers. CR.
WilliamsonMusic publication and allied rts. UBP, ARR

Publications Copyrights

© 1 1989 UBP New American Library, division of Penguin Books USA, Inc .

© 2 1971 UBP Fleming H. Revell Company

© 3 1986 UBP Rawson Associates, imprint Macmillan Publishing Co.

© 4 1985 UBP New American Library, division of Penguin Books USA, Inc.

© 5 1987 UBP Doubleday, division of Bantam Doubleday Dell Publishing Group, Inc.

© 6 1991 UBP St. Martins Pres

© 7 1991 UBP Villard Publications, division of Random House

© 8 1982 UBP Putnam Publishing Group

© 9 1983 UBP Doubleday, Division of Bantam Doubleday Dell Publishing Group, Inc.

© 10 1986 UBP McGraw Hill Book Company